DAILY HOMILIES
Ordinary Time — Year I

ST PAULS

Library of Congress Cataloging-in-Publication Data

Krempa, S. Joseph.
   Daily homilies.

   Contents: v. 1. Ordinary Time—year I;
v. 2. Ordinary Time—year II;
v. 3. Seasonal and sanctoral, Advent, Christmas,
Lent & Easter, and all obligatory memorials.
   1. Catholic Church—Sermons. 2. Sermons—American.
3. Christian saints—Biography.   I. Title.
BX1756.K782D34   1984   252'.6   84-24224
ISBN 0-8189-0480-1 (vol. I)
ISBN 0-8189-0481-X (vol. II)
ISBN 0-8189-0479-8 (vol. III)
ISBN 0-8189-0483-6 (set)

Nihil Obstat:
Rev. Thomas E. Crane

Imprimatur:
✠ Most Rev. Edward D. Head
Bishop of Buffalo
November 13, 1984

Produced and designed in the United States of America by the
Fathers and Brothers of the Society of St. Paul,
2187 Victory Boulevard, Staten Island, New York 10314-6603
as part of their communications apostolate.

Printing Information:

Current Printing - first digit   6   7   8   9   10

Year of Current Printing - first year shown

          2001 2002 2003 2004 2005 2006 2007 2008 2009 2010

DAILY HOMILIES
Ordinary Time — Year I

by

Rev. S. Joseph Krempa

In Three Volumes

Volume 1   Ordinary Time—Year I
Volume 2   Ordinary Time—Year II
Volume 3   Seasonal & Sanctoral

A L B A · H O U S E   alba house   N E W · Y O R K

SOCIETY OF ST. PAUL, 2187 VICTORY BLVD., STATEN ISLAND. NEW YORK 10314

PREFACE

During the week, a Mass celebrant encounters three groups of people: those who come daily, others who attend regularly and some who participate occasionally. A homilist has an obligation to each of these groups. One writer has compared it to preaching to a parade. Each day's scriptural selection is presented here with an exegetical and theological integrity of its own. Thematic unity for daily participants is balanced, however, by regular summaries so that the needs of the occasional participant are not disregarded.

The liturgical sense — the spiritual message as proclaimed — dominates these homilies although their deep background is based on technical analysis. A five minute reflection cannot be an occasion for a proper discussion of chiastic structure, Lukan sutures and the various levels of biblical criticism for people whose interests are more immediate and personal. Excellent and useful treatments of scriptural literary analysis abound, thankfully.

At the conclusion of this lengthy work, some important acknowledgments are necessary. I would like to thank Archbishop Thomas Kelly of Louisville, Kentucky for his inspiration and example; Rev. Vincent Donovan of Laurel, Maryland for his discursive, but always insightful, Monday morning conversations; the Woodstock Theological Center Library at Georgetown University in Washington, D.C. for the generous permission to use their collection; special thanks to the community at the daily evening Mass at St. Nicholas Church in Laurel, Maryland whose patience, faith and encouragement made this book possible.

A distinct word of gratitude to my Ordinary, Bishop Edward Head of Buffalo, New York for his kindness. He is a man of extraordinary common sense who, over the past decade, has healed a diocese. Through his deep trust in everything Catholic, he has made Western New York a home for a wide, lively and diverse Catholic family.

Rev. S. Joseph Krempa

to Rev. Eugene Weber,
priest of West Virginia,
magnificent pastor,
sure guide on the Christian journey
who brings the Word to life every day

MONDAY — First Week of the Year
Heb 1:1-6   *Mk 1:14-20*

First Reading

The Letter to the Hebrews is the only analysis of the priesthood of Jesus Christ in the entire New Testament. By a fresh and searching examination of who Jesus was and what He accomplished, the unknown author (who, for the sake of convenience, we will call *Hebrews*) tries to inject new life into the faith of Jewish (or Essene) Christians who were on the brink of spiritual burnout.

Hebrews begins with a magnificent sweep of pre-Christian faith. "In the past, God spoke to our fathers in fragmentary and varied ways. . . ." As a matter of fact, not even the Old Testament exhausts the entire story of God's word to mankind because there is no culture to which God is a total stranger. "But now, He has spoken through His Son, the perfect copy of the Father's being." Because of His deep intimacy with and access to the Father, Jesus is the magnet toward which all the slivers of truth scattered in various religions and cultures are attracted. He is the full and final Word of God who now lives in the Church and through our faith and love.

Gospel Reading

Jesus begins His ministry in Galilee, a place which Mark almost lyrically identifies with faith. As Jesus calls people to an innovative way of living and experiencing God, hundreds of prophetic promises come to a climax. The disciples' response to the call of Jesus is prompt and complete. Mark's Gospel is about discipleship. The rest of the Gospel will illustrate the personal and public implications of our accepting or rejecting the dominion of God.

The Lord has not been silent in our lives. By unpacking the moment when we first began to take our faith seriously, we will discern the time when, back in our "Galilee," Jesus looked at each of us to say, "Come with me!" And we did.

Point

We are not called to pattern our lives on abstractions but on the living Christ.

TUESDAY — First Week of the Year
Heb 2:5-12   *Mk 1:21-28*

First Reading

The first reading describes the Lordship of Jesus in terms of His supremacy over angels, forces, spirits and powers. "The world was not designed to be subject to angels . . . but to people." The human personality is the most valuable item of creation. The drama of mankind's struggle with faith and love gives greater glory to the power of God than does any natural vista. Human beings are designed to be the apex and fulfillment of creation, but the world in which we live does not evidence that. Bureaucratic, economic and political forces, wildly out of control, seem to dehumanize and overpower individuals. Although mankind is not yet in full mastery of creation, God's original design has begun to come true in the risen Christ. Jesus is now what we were born to become.

Gospel Reading

The first sign of Jesus' power in Mark's Gospel is an exorcism. Jesus came with more than a message or alternative religious option. He brought a power and release from our spiritual and moral debilities. He broke the back of evil for us. His confrontations with the power of darkness both in His ministry and on the cross reveal how the shadow side of life became the instrument of His Resurrection and glory.

We know that personal failure can be the start of a new direction for us. The experience of sin can enable us to appreciate the gift of forgiveness and spiritual rebirth. Jesus is our Lord not because He descended in glory from heaven but because He entered the very bowels of human life and forged there a full expression of His Sonship.

Point

Jesus was not perfected in spite of His suffering but rather through it.

WEDNESDAY — First Week of the Year
Heb 2:14-18   *Mk 1:29-39*

First Reading

Today's first reading presents another reason for the Lordship of Jesus: His ability to transmit His risen power to us.

Jesus was not a passive victim in the teeth of evil. If He had come simply to endure pain, the healings throughout the Gospels would be inexplicable. Jesus confronted evil by letting the Father live and work through Him. The heart of Jesus' obedience to the Father was the full transparency of every cell of His being to God wherever that might lead — to public honor or to the torture of crucifixion.

To face down evil and pain, whether in the forms of emotional problems, illness or unemployment is never easy. Jesus came to enable us to let the Father live and work through us.

Gospel Reading

Jesus restores Peter's mother-in-law to a full and productive life. His message to us is that our deepest fulfillment is
found in allowing the Father to work through our intelligence,
abilities, imagination and personalities. Communicating that
message of the liberation available to us when we submit to the
rule of God was more crucial to the Lord than attracting crowds
through miracles. Whenever His demonstrations of God's
kingship distract from that primary message, Jesus moves to
another town as He does in today's reading.

Point

*The real miracle is our coming to a realization that God
continues the work of creation through us.*

THURSDAY — First Week of the Year
Heb 3:7-14   *Mk 1:40-45*

First Reading

To recharge faith in Jesus, *Hebrews* has emphasized that
Jesus is Lord because He perfectly reflects the Father, fulfills
God's design for creation and can transmit His risen life to us.
We should recall that the crisis facing the readers or hearers of
Hebrews was not an intellectual one. It was probably the
malaise of spiritual lethargy.

A classic image describing the Christian life is the Exodus
model of our departure from the grip of sin through the waters
of Baptism. Our promised land is enduring happiness in God's
presence. Between our exodus and its fulfillment is the travel-
ling time of faith — the Christian life — where enthusiasm
easily wanes. Appropriately, *Hebrews* refers to the Old Testa-

ment incident at Meribah where the thirsty Israelites demanded miraculous water from God. God judged that generation unprepared for the freedom of the promised land because their dependence on continual divine intervention blinded them to His presence in the ordinary contours of daily life.

Gospel Reading

A leper, banished by Law, is cleansed by Jesus as the townspeople start to promote not Jesus' teaching but His miracles. One can become enticed by a magical view of faith that divorces miracle from message and searches exclusively for extraordinary phenomena while failing to see the work of God in the broad movements of ordinary life. The eventual result is a spiritual drift from a God seen to be inaccessible. Fidelity requires an effort to integrate faith with our daily experience to avoid a two-track existence where religion shrinks into either a quick fix for intractable situations or a miraculous punctuation of an otherwise agnostic life style.

Point

Faithfulness is much more than the avoidance of heresy. It is the cultivation of an adult spiritual life.

FRIDAY — First Week of the Year
Heb 4:1-5, 11   *Mk 2:1-12*

First Reading

The Exodus motif pervades this first reading's description of the promised land as a geographical version of the Sabbath rest. Genesis had traced the Sabbath to the very start of creation. It was part of the natural order. The Sabbath reminds us that we were made for more than simply work by pointing to a future when every person will stand freely in the dignity of a son or daughter of God.

For many people, the Sabbath is simply another free day. In an environment of powerful secularizing forces, the residue of a lost Christian life style is only an occasional reference to God. Such casual believers, *Hebrews* asserts, will never know the "rest" of God. They will never experience God as the quiet center of their lives.

Gospel Reading

Jesus begins to clash with entrenched religious power. While Jesus was at home (His own? another's?), the faith of friends precipitated a paralyzed man's cure. One of the strands woven into Mark's Gospel is a polemic against an image of Jesus as one of many wandering miracle workers. In this reading Jesus cures the man to prove to the incredulous Pharisees that a more profound and significant healing had taken place in the forgiveness of sin. "So that you will know that the Son of Man has power to forgive sins, I command you, rise and walk." The miracles were evidences of the spiritual regeneration at work in the kingdom of God and not vice versa.

Point

Once we are reconciled with God and others, pieces of our life begin to fall into place.

SATURDAY — First Week of the Year
Heb 4:12-16   *Mk 2:13-17*

First Reading

The Word of God is described as "alive and active." This phrase refers not only to the Bible but also has a much wider meaning. It refers to the Word of God spoken to creation and embodied in the laws of nature; it is the Word of God spoken through the prophets and embodied in the laws of justice and fair dealing; it is the Word of God spoken in Jesus Christ and embodied in the living tradition and liturgy of the Church.

Hebrews warns us not to trifle with this Word because it has another edge as a Word of judgment. There are measurable, empirical consequences if we abuse our planet, ignore massive social injustice or disregard the Word of life offered to us in Jesus. Such neglect receives the same judgment as apostasy and heresy because the result is identical. They all choke off the Spirit.

Gospel Reading

Jesus dines with tax collectors, a sector of society despised as social pariahs. According to the strict law of the Old Testament, commerce with such public sinners made an individual ritually unclean. It was guilt by association with a vengeance. Jesus cracks open the status quo as He draws people into the kingdom who, until now, had been excluded. Jesus cleansed, healed and changed an assortment of outsiders such as Levi. Ritual uncleanness may have had some logic when ritual effectiveness was a function of a devotee's personal holiness and the power to forgive was seen to be lodged in a remote God. Now, however, the power to forgive which moves among us is the person of Jesus. He is Messiah — our abiding agent of reconciliation and the source of liturgical power.

Point

Jesus is more than an example of kindness. He is the very energy of God reconciling us to the Father.

MONDAY — Second Week of the Year
Heb 5:1-10   *Mk 2:18-22*

First Reading

The Letter to the Hebrews is one of the most compelling and profound statements about the mystery of Jesus which, ironically, is shrouded in an obscure Judaeo-Hellenistic frame of reference remote from our own. The organizing theme of *Hebrews* with which we can identify is the priesthood of Jesus Christ. People have always searched for some way of contacting God, however they named Him. They set aside certain places, times and officials as intermediaries between themselves and God. We need a bridge builder to span the moral and psychological distance we experience between ourselves and God.

Hebrews argues not only that Jesus is such a mediator, but that He is the only real and effective one. Every part of Jesus — emotions, body, intelligence and will power — was completely penetrated by the Holy Spirit. In Jesus was born a new human way of being, completely receptive to God's power. God and humanity are bonded once and for all in Christ. That new way of being human became a possibility for all of us in the Resurrection.

Gospel Reading

We grasp the distinction between Testaments in the difference between John and Jesus. John's disciples fasted and did penance to reach out to God. In Jesus, God reaches out into our hearts and lives. The Lord describes this as fresh, new wine. Just as the pressure from the fermentation of new grapes would explode old wineskins, so the new incarnated presence of Jesus would burst out of the old Jewish institutions from which it began. This new wine means that everything now is built on Christ. He is the Temple, the Bread of Life, the Living Water, the

Light of the World, the Passover. Jesus' presence renders all things holy. Secondly, Christ's work of reconciliation is dynamic. The work of drawing mankind back to God continues to expand through our lives as Christians.

Point

Because of Jesus, we are now as far from God as we choose to be.

TUESDAY — Second Week of the Year
Heb 6:10-20 *Mk 2:23-28*

First Reading

The author, *Hebrews*, steps aside briefly from the priesthood theme to encourage his backsliding readers. Spiritual enthusiasm can be sustained if we have some kind of certainty that God will bring us to the goal He has promised. Such confidence does not float in mid-air but is based on God's past performance. We can look to Abraham's experience of God and God's "oath" to make a great nation from this man of faith. Today, three great religious traditions call Abraham their father in faith. We can look to the Church's experience of God and the Lord's promise that it will survive in power. We can look to Jesus' experience of the Father. The reality of His Resurrection was so over-powering that it remodeled the thinking of the first disciples. Finally, we can look to our own experience of God over the past decade to see His presence in our personal story.

Gospel Reading

Another controversy arises — this one about the Sabbath. Jesus does not negate the holiness of the Sabbath but how reverence for it was expressed. These words of Jesus had special meaning for those early Christians who shifted their Sabbath celebration to Sunday after they had been excluded from the synagogue. Beneath this controversy and the bold confidence of the early Christians in rearranging their worship obligations is the recognition of Jesus as the source and animating spirit of religious law and practice. Without the Holy Spirit of Christ, religious law can easily become a burden and engine of sin.

Point

The things for which we hope influence what we are today.

WEDNESDAY — Second Week of the Year
Heb 7:1-3, 15-17   *Mk 3:1-6*

First Reading

We rejoin the discussion of Jesus' priesthood. Melchizedek is a puzzling figure out of the Book of Genesis. Some writers have compared the envelope of mystery surrounding Melchizedek to that mist of uncertainty that hides the sources of the Letter to the Hebrews. Apparently, he was king of Salem (Jerusalem) and a priest of God. His origin and later whereabouts were unknown. Yet, Abraham reverenced him. *Hebrews* uses this enigmatic figure to make a point about the priesthood of Jesus. Like Melchizedek, Jesus did not inherit His priesthood because He was not from the priestly tribe of Levi. Jesus was made a priest by God, just as Melchizedek was according to Genesis. Therefore, Jesus' ancestry is irrelevant because His priesthood does not derive from His tribal heritage but from the power of His indestructible Resurrection life. Easter is the source of Jesus' eternal priestly power to link us with God.

Gospel Reading

The Sabbath issue flares up once more. By examining the purpose of work, Jesus answers the charge that work is absolutely prohibited on the Sabbath. The Law cannot forbid doing good. Such a result would fatally confuse means and ends. In refocusing the meaning of Law and covenant, Jesus is a true priest as He clarifies our understanding of the Law and urges us toward an adult faith.

At the end of this brief but fundamental controversy, we sense that the clock is ticking. For opposing entrenched views and vested interests, death is now on Jesus' horizon. Neither His priesthood nor our discipleship would be bloodless.

Point

The function of any priest is, first of all, to help us see the Father rather than to only tell us about Him.

THURSDAY — Second Week of the Year
Heb 7:25-8:6   *Mk 3:7-12*

First Reading

Hebrews now begins to trace a trajectory of contrasts through priesthoods, covenants, temples and rituals. Some have written that *Hebrews* is trying to head off a relapse into Jewish liturgy or a nostalgic theological recidivism in the early Church which allegorized Jewish liturgical practices.

This reading compares the Old Testament priesthood with that of Jesus. Under the Old Law, the tribe of Levi had hundreds of priestly families repeating annual cycles of rituals. In Jesus we have only one priest, made such by God, who offered His life as a unique, dynamic, perpetually fruitful sacrifice. *Hebrews* uses the framework of the Levitical priesthood to make two major points. First, the passion, death and Resurrection of Jesus is not only an historical event but a source of continuing power. Secondly, the Resurrection is not only Christ's personal victory but ours as well. Jesus died once and for everyone.

It is difficult for non-Catholics to appreciate that the celebration of the Eucharist is not a supplementary addition to Jesus' sacrifice. Rather, the moment and power of Jesus' death and Resurrection are captured sacramentally and made available to us through the liturgy. The Paschal Mystery is an active spiritual volcano.

Gospel Reading

In contrast to yesterday's reading about a handful of scheming Pharisees, today's Gospel reading portrays the crowds that followed the Lord. Place names are important here. Mark is writing for a community which is a mix of Jewish and Gentile Christians. He reminds them that the crowds which sought Jesus out were from larger Jewish and Gentile population centers. As Jesus continues to teach and heal, we perceive a gradual transformation of the old Israel into a new and expanded Israel which He gently and gradually shapes through word and deed.

Through our celebration of the Eucharist, Jesus continues to extend His embrace as He builds and molds His people.

Point

At different seasons we discover deeper meanings in the life, death and rising of the Lord.

FRIDAY — Second Week of the Year
Heb 8:6-13   *Mk 3:13-19*

First Reading

The first reading compares the old and new covenants. The old covenant governed human behavior but was powerless to enable people to live according to its requirements. It could not pluck out the source of sin within us. It was simply a preparatory stage to a new covenant which would finally enable us not only to act as, but to be, children and people of God.

Jesus is the priest and agent of this new arrangement. We become a brand new creation through Him. The vision of Jeremiah which looked forward to a deeper intimacy between God and people has come true in Jesus. Creation took a quantum leap in Christ because the link between God and people is no longer simply Law but Spirit. In human hearts the Spirit takes up His rest.

Gospel Reading

Jesus selects the Twelve and gives them His messianic power. Some gifts of the Lord were given to the entire Church; others were given to the apostolic college alone.

We all share in the priesthood of Jesus in different ways. The "priesthood of the laity" means that all baptized persons have received the Holy Spirit and have direct access to the Father. Knowledge of God and the experience of His love are not limited to a special few. This carries in turn a special responsibility for others. As the new people of God, we are all called to bridge and heal the gaps between people and to enable them to realize their bondedness to God.

Point

Even though we do not wear vestments, we are all priests of the new covenant created by Christ.

SATURDAY — Second Week of the Year
Heb 9:2-3, 11-14   *Mk 3:20-21*

First Reading

The holy tent built in the desert was an awesome sight. In the center of a series of rooms was the holiest of holy places, the one spot on earth where the Jewish people were certain God could be reached. The high priest stepped into this place only once a year to approach God on behalf of the people. In Jesus' day, the Holy of Holies was in the Temple of Jerusalem. *Hebrews* tells us that the Risen Lord stepped into a sanctuary far more perfect than tent or temple. He entered the very glory of God. As a result, we have through Jesus an ongoing source of freedom, renewal and forgiveness as vigorous and fresh as it was on that first Easter morning. This is much more than Israel's annual Day of Atonement for past wrongs. Jesus can rejuvenate our hearts, that holiest spot deep inside a person where we are genuinely made whole.

Gospel Reading

Forgiveness . . . liberation . . . reconciliation! It was difficult to imagine such things happening without elaborate temple rituals. Yet, these are precisely the events taking place in the first three chapters of Mark's Gospel. The crowds were enthralled; Jesus' relatives were nonplussed; the Pharisees bristled with hate. Jesus was claiming the very power attributed to the exalted rituals of the Temple and much more. He was the healing presence of God. We in turn will experience the same variety of reactions from others the more closely we follow the Lord.

Point

All the power of ritual, prayer and priesthood derives from Jesus and leads back to Him.

MONDAY — Third Week of the Year
Heb 9:15, 24-28   *Mk 3:22-30*

First Reading

Hebrews contrasts the sanctuaries we build as access points to God with the domain of God into which Jesus has fully entered. Ancient religions and modern therapies try to express in shrine and symbol what Jesus achieved in fact. When Jesus went into the presence and glory of the Father, all the prayers, works, joys and sufferings of His life were glorified as well because they are inextricably part of Him. They compose the life and person that the Father found to be entirely and uniquely acceptable.

Our works and sufferings share this same redemptive value when we unite them with those of Christ. The Father sees and loves in us what He sees and loves in Jesus.

Gospel Reading

Scribes had come down from Jerusalem and charged Jesus with being a Satanic agent. Their logic was linear and one dimensional. He had been observed transgressing the Law and was therefore legally unclean. His miracles, then, could not be from God. Of course, Jesus did not violate the Law in its

profound sense. He fulfilled it. He breached rabbinic conven-
tion and questioned the interpretation of the Law, but not the
Law's own validity. His exorcisms indicate the collapse of
Satan's rule. Jesus broke into the house of Satan to rescue the
captives trapped inside. Jesus turns around the Pharisees' accusation of sin to remind them that their refusal to recognize the
obvious works of God is the unforgivable sin. A perversion of
mind that calls darkness light and interprets light as darkness is
unforgivable because it has cannibalized conscience and
reason, a person's lifelines to truth.

Point

*Conscience and reason are the traces of God within us.
When they are energized by the Holy Spirit, the road to new life
begins.*

TUESDAY — Third Week of the Year
Heb 10:1-10   *Mk 3:31-35*

First Reading

Let us summarize the argument of this tenth chapter of the
Letter to the Hebrews. The entire system of Jewish law and
liturgy was only a silhouette of what Jesus would do. The
annual repetitions of sacrifices under the old system could
never save or remove the source of sin. In fact, the very opposite occurred. These yearly rituals reminded people of the
ineradicability of sin just as temples and priesthoods under-
scored their distance from God. In short, the blood of bulls
could not wash sin away. In the new covenant, wherein Christ
gave His own life to the Father, we are forgiven and cleansed
inside and out. Christianity does not seek simply to tranquilize
the effects of sin but to strike at its root. The goal of all other

religions had been attained in Jesus' single comprehensive act on Calvary.

Gospel Reading

Jesus describes the spiritual nature of our link to God. Faith places us within a new network of relationships to each other, Himself and to the Father. As the theologians used to say: we become by gift what Jesus was by nature. His connections become our own. By hearing and complementing the words of Christ we are assimilated to a new level of experience and life because the same life that infused Jesus now flows between the Father and us and draws us to each other. This spiritual community is absolutely vital as a support network in the very difficult life of discipleship.

Point

Our baptism is a permanent source of spiritual vitality.

WEDNESDAY — Third Week of the Year
Heb 10:11-18   *Mk 4:1-20*

First Reading

The professional priests of the old Law offered rounds of rituals to placate, atone to and plead with God. The temples that dot South America and Africa are monuments to mankind's transcultural experience of sin and the universal quest for release from its crippling effects. It was not in a temple but through His own life that Jesus offered the only completely perfect sacrifice of human history that defanged sin's mortal power from the heart and soul of mankind. That single act of Jesus was so complete that it is a source of forgiveness for everybody. It is not the brutality of the crucifixion but the thoroughness of Jesus' lifetime obedience to the Father that powers our forgiveness.

Gospel Reading

The Lord presents a parable which was esteemed very much by the early Church. The parable of the sower explains why His own did not accept Him and describes various responses to the Gospel met by the early Christians: the shallow mind, the hard heart, the easily diverted and the morally weak. None of us is naturally able to give initially a total response to the Gospel call. There are pockets of resistance in our minds, emotions and habits. These are not necessarily areas of sin but of guarded immaturity. By faith, we can slowly begin to draw down the power and light of Jesus into the most recalcitrant areas of our life. This is one great challenge of discipleship: to give our faith concrete expression in our professional, sexual, economic and leisure activities.

Point

Faith is a process as much as it is an act.

THURSDAY — Third Week of the Year
Heb 10:19-25   *Mk 4:21-25*

First Reading

Jesus' sacrifice was so total and sweeping that it was exhaustive. Nothing more is needed. Because of that, we can now walk right into the Holy of Holies. Jesus has opened the curtain not only for the high priest but for everyone — bus drivers, bricklayers, secretaries, teachers — to enter. This is the fresh, new life-giving way He has opened into the very presence of God. We can have the same easy intimacy with the Father which Jesus has. This access we have been given is strengthened by our celebration of the Eucharist which enables us to keep our new avenue to God wide open.

Gospel Reading

An odd saying: those who have will receive more; those without much will have even more taken away. Continuing indifference to the Gospel can harden our hearts and lead to a loss of insight. Our capacity for spiritual insight is deepened by the Holy Spirit as we continue to improve our access to God. Liturgy links us to a larger community of prayer with its own rhythms and moods to balance our spiritual life. To cut ourselves off from this movement of prayer will not simply freeze us where we are. It will lead to decline and spiritual atrophy.

Point

We must work to keep open the access to the Father that the Lord Jesus has given us.

FRIDAY — Third Week of the Year
Heb 10:32-39   *Mk 4:26-34*

First Reading

Hebrews reminds the Jewish Christians (who were probably in a hiatus between persecutions) of the heroic endurance they, or their parents, had shown in the past. We all have instances of great exercise of faith in our past when we were young or first converted. The Lord seemed so close then and the Christian life seemed to be a great adventure of faith. Then, as time passed, we slipped away. We might look back wistfully on that early faith as gone forever.

The faith and devotion we then knew were fresh and untried. Just as the early love of a newly-married couple can mature as years pass, so the energy of faith can mature and become part of the texture of our lives over time. Experience can strip away our illusions and enable us to see clearly the strong and weak elements of that early faith of ours. Time need not erode but can refine faith.

Gospel Reading

Like the mustard seed that grows into a great tree, the beginnings of faith are small. This image illustrates the enormous potential locked into our baptismal grace. With the passage of time and the grace of the Holy Spirit, circumstances reveal the power of that faith. The devastation of sickness, for example, can make us aware of depths to our faith and trust in God that we never previously realized were there. The great saints of history were not endowed at their baptism with more of the Holy Spirit than we were. But they did let that Spirit pervade their lives more thoroughly than we might have.

Point

Circumstances can reveal the enormous potential of our faith and love.

SATURDAY — Third Week of the Year
Heb 11:1-2, 8-19   *Mk 4:35-41*

First Reading

We come to a famous chapter of the Letter to the Hebrews: the roll call of the saints. *Hebrews* lists great people of faith —

Abraham, Isaac, Jacob — all of whom lived their lives hoping for the promised fullness of God's presence that we have been given. Relying only on inspirations and prophetic words, they never came to the promised land of the Holy Spirit, the Jerusalem of the Spirit-filled life that Jesus made available to us. All of them died believing and hoping. Yet that hope enabled them to endure great trials. The everyday access to God that we have was, for them, only an aspiration. For us it is a real and sacramental experience.

Gospel Reading

The miracle of the calming of the storm was preserved by the early Church not simply because it was a memorable event. This incident, in fact, is a graphic description of the Marcan community. They were experiencing unpopularity, persecution and death. Their faith was severely strained. Mark uses this incident to show the disciples' lack of trust in Jesus even though He was with them physically. The Lord is with us sacramentally as we eat His Body and drink His Blood. The failure to completely trust the Lord is an abiding temptation for us as well. We need the help of the Holy Spirit to keep faith in any storm.

Point

The real threat of any storm is the temptation to believe the Lord has abandoned us. Faith assures us that He is with us — even in the storm.

MONDAY — Fourth Week of the Year
Heb 11:32-40   *Mk 5:1-20*

First Reading

This reading from the celebrated eleventh chapter of the Letter to the Hebrews is a powerful appeal for faith not as a body of beliefs but as trust and assurance that God cares. Most of us have difficulty with such faith as did the recipients of this circulating letter. It recites a litany of the accomplishments of ancient heroes: Gideon, Barak, Samson, etc. He tells us they did not receive what they were promised until Christ came. If they were able to achieve so much, what greater things should we be able to accomplish. We can contemporize this argument slightly. We have a greater availability of religious resources than did the generations before us. Yet, with limited economic and political influence, our predecessors built up the magnificent infrastructure of the American Church. Their achievement remains a benchmark for us.

Gospel Reading

Jesus is in pagan territory. After expelling some unusually powerful demons in a case of possession, He does not silence their address to Him as "Son of the Most High." Perhaps here in Gentile territory there was little danger of the politicization of His Messiahship. Upon releasing the man, Jesus sends him back to his family. This exemplifies a way faith can be built up and strengthened — by sharing with others our experiences of God's work in our lives. This is something we Catholics are not in the habit of doing. Keeping such stories private squanders a tremendous opportunity to graphically and realistically display how faith takes shape in human life not back in Galilee but here and now.

Point

The sharing of faith stories constitutes a faith community.

TUESDAY — Fourth Week of the Year

Heb 12:1-4   *Mk 5:21-43*

First Reading

Hebrews continues to call his vacillating readers to fidelity. Yesterday, we heard the litany of past heroes and were reminded of their achievements. Today, we have a striking new image: the race of life. *Hebrews* pictures the past generations of God's faithful ones of both Testaments gathered in a stadium urging us to run the race. We can imagine them applauding and shouting words of encouragement. It is a dynamic picture of the communion of saints.

He also suggests how to keep faith alive. Don't get trapped in the present. Look ahead. Follow Jesus our "coach." Get rid of whatever holds you back. See everything that happens to you as "training." Use it to build up faith. Above all, keep your eye on the goal.

Gospel Reading

At first, both Jairus and the woman who spent her life savings on doctors wanted physical contact with Jesus — a touch of the garment, a laying on of hands. In both cases, Jesus looked beneath the surface touch to the deeper contact of faith. Through faith we make contact with the Lord. There is no advantage to those who touched His cloak back in Galilee twenty centuries ago. We can contact the same Jesus and be healed by the same saving power through faith and the sacramental, liturgical life of the Church.

Point

Faith perceives the very real spiritual connections laced throughout our world into God.

WEDNESDAY — Fourth Week of the Year
Heb 12:4-7, 11-15   *Mk 6:1-6*

First Reading

Hebrews reminds his readers that although they have not been called to full martyrdom, they have still been tested. The very problems they are experiencing can become tools of self-renewal. By facing down its difficulties, a parish community can come to a deeper appreciation of the real bases of its identity and the significance of its faith. Struggles and conflicts crack open the thin veneer of superficial fellow-feeling with which we can easily become content. They expose not only the real wounds but the profound and subtle points of unity in a parish. *Hebrews* encourages us to strive after peace and holiness and to root out any residual bitterness that, left unexpressed and unattended, can pollute our achievements.

Gospel Reading

Jesus had been too familiar to His townspeople. His words, background and family were well-known to them. As He walked their streets, they probably continued their business without giving Him any special attention. They may have seen Him as teacher or rabbi, but not as Lord. The same can happen with our faith as it did with the readers of the Letter to the Hebrews. The faith and the Church can become so familiar that the drama of what it means to be a follower of Christ can be lost. As the Pope once stated compactly: "When it is hard to be Christian, it is easy to be Christian. When it is easy to be Christian, it is hard to be Christian." Prosperity can cause us to lose sight of the powerful and liberating realities represented by words such as "redemption," "forgiveness," and "resurrection." In such circumstances, problems and difficulties can reconfigure a familiar faith and bring the ancient words to new life.

Point

The crises of faith can generate a fresh start to our faith.

THURSDAY — Fourth Week of the Year
Heb 12:18-19, 21-24   *Mk 6:7-13*

First Reading

This first reading summarizes the argument of the entire Letter to the Hebrews. The contrast between Mount Sinai and Mount Zion should not be interpreted as confirmation of the false and timeworn contrast between the vengeful God of the Old Testament and the loving God of the New Testament. It is not a change in God's nature but a shift in our understanding of God. This God of love was dimly perceived by people of old in fragmentary and varied ways. Now, the avenue to God is wide open through the new and living way Jesus created. There is no going back! Now we are able to enjoy a degree of communion with God which all the machinery of the ancient sacrificial system tried in vain to attain. For this very reason, much more is expected of us.

Gospel Reading

Jesus instructs His missionaries to shake the dust of a town from their feet and move on if the people refuse to listen to the message. Frequently, however, a fallen believer can become so hardhearted that he or she is more immune to the power of God's Word than a person who has never heard the Gospel in the first place. Such individuals cut themselves off from an entire spiritual dimension of life and reality — the only dimension, *Hebrews* reminds us, that abides. To evangelize the fallen-away is extremely difficult because they have been anesthetized to the impact of God's Word. For all sorts of reasons, that inner center deep within them where God and creature can meet has been shut tight against intrusion. Such individuals might never come to appreciate the truth about themselves and God.

Point

God's love is not a toy. Its acceptance brings life and its refusal brings spiritual death.

FRIDAY — Fourth Week of the Year
Heb 13:1-8   *Mk 6:14-29*

First Reading

The soaring theological document we call the Letter to the Hebrews ends with a series of moral exhortations. "Do not neglect to show hospitality." It reminds us of the importance to a community not only of heroic deeds but of day to day consideration for others. Christian kindness should not be triggered only by a major crisis. Simple civility is the software on which a parish regularly operates. Basic manners are the oil that allows a community to continue functioning. Powerful experiences of Christian community do not spring into being from nowhere. They need a base from which to come.

Gospel Reading

The Baptist's death coincides with the first mission of the disciples just as the Church's mission will follow the death of Jesus. The story of John's death is placed here to advert to the shadow of the cross that is darkening the ministry of Jesus. John would be Jesus' predecessor in preaching as well as in suffering. *Hebrews* told us to remember the courage of our leaders. When we live and speak the Gospel clearly and directly, we are most like Jesus in His ministry, suffering and hidden glory. The shadow of the cross is always on the horizon of the Church's work. Church workers die and pass to the Father every day, and sometimes violently. But Jesus is the same yesterday, today and tomorrow. He remains the center of the Church to give energy and drive to a parish's life across many generations.

Point

We reflect Jesus not only in heroism but in everyday life.

SATURDAY — Fourth Week of the Year
Heb 13:15-17, 20-21   *Mk 6:30-34*

First Reading

The Letter to the Hebrews concludes with simple admonitions for a healthy community life. Our daily life is the material of the ongoing offering we make to the Father. The life of a parish or family is joined with Christ's single great transcendent sacrifice through us. Everyday life can be as arduous and difficult, in its own way, as the great moments of martyrdom. The rush of adrenalin in a crisis is far preferable to the deadening boredom of routine. Yet, just as Jesus' daily life was completed on the cross, so our daily routine is the stuff of our offering and the instrument of our holiness.

Gospel Reading

The crowds were like sheep without a shepherd. On a level deeper than verbal instruction, Jesus gives direction to our individual and parish lives through His Spirit. To the extent that a community is open to the Lord, it will receive direction from Him not in a thunderclap but through prayerful consensus. He is the great high priest who connects us into the life of the Father and into the Father's design for creation. Through Jesus, our parishes and individual lives participate in the great drama of salvation history.

Point

The great work of Jesus continues in our daily and seemingly uneventful lives.

MONDAY — Fifth Week of the Year
Gn 1:1-19   *Mk 6:53-56*

First Reading

The Book of Genesis will be the source of our first reading for the next two weeks. While everyone knows what Genesis says, it is easy to overlook its meaning. This magnificent affirmation of Jewish faith reached its final form about 500 years before Christ. It is a brilliant weave of ancient traditions from northern, southern and priestly circles assembled during the exile to counter yet another gathering spiritual crisis. Women were degraded; the covenant was disregarded; the Sabbath was ignored; pagan practices were being assimilated. Genesis speaks to the spiritual crisis of its time and of any age by telling a story that goes back to the beginning. A careful reading of Genesis will actually tell us more about God's covenant with Israel and the enduring problems of civilization than it does about the dawn of creation.

Today's first reading makes several points. While pagan myths saw a world born out of primeval conflict, the God of Israel creates effortlessly with a Word. The God of Israel and of the covenant is not another local deity but Lord of the universe. The sun, stars and fertility which pagans worshipped were created by the God of Sinai to serve humanity. Finally, all of creation was good — every bit of it.

Gospel Reading

The Lord's healings indicate that suffering and evil are not God's curse laid upon us. The world as created by God is not evil but good. Disorder is the product of sin and distance from the Creator. Yet, the Bible teaches how the widening split of sin is met by an increasingly focused power of grace. From Genesis through Christ, the Scriptures describe the gradual process of restoration, rescue and re-creation.

Point

In the Bible, we witness a great cycle of creation back to God: ransomed, healed, restored and forgiven.

TUESDAY — Fifth Week of the Year
Gn 1:20-2:4   *Mk 7:1-13*

First Reading

This reading from Genesis presents us with a powerful religious vision evolved over generations in the priestly tradition and recrafted through experience and crisis. Yesterday, we saw the first part of this story of creation composed to counteract a slow slide into pagan forms of worship. Its point was to show that the world was created not to be worshipped but to be enjoyed. To so demythologize the world was an important breakthrough in locating divinity where it properly belongs. Only Yahweh is God.

Today's reading continues the poem by portraying mankind as the capstone of creation. God creates mankind in "our" likeness, i.e. of God and the created world. Man is the link between heaven and earth. We resemble God in our intelligence, free will, creativity and love. The creation of mankind as male and female indicates that sexual attraction is not a deviation from God's creative design but its extension. "Dominion" is not a license to exploit but a mandate to care for the planet. Finally, by keeping the Sabbath we imitate our Creator God and remind ourselves that creation is to be also a place of rest. This seventh day is holy and without morning or evening. The human being has become God's vicar on earth.

Gospel Reading

Religious traditions make life coherent and insert us into a wide community of faith and meaning. These traditions were turned by some Jewish teachers into a bludgeon to generate guilt and evasive techniques. The Korban was a loophole: "Declare it holy so you can keep it." Religion slowly became an instrument of self-deception and neurosis. In contrast to the Pharisees who were watching, spying, measuring, distinguishing, categorizing, legalizing and turning the Sabbath and life into a game of religious "hide and seek," Jesus restores the commanding vision of Genesis where life is a gift from God to be reverenced and celebrated.

Point

We must work to keep God's world and Christ's community uncorrupted.

WEDNESDAY — Fifth Week of the Year
Gn 2:5-9,15-17   Mk 7:14-23

First Reading

Today's first reading describes a second creation story. The prior story, the six-day account, was a magnificent priestly reflection on the sovereignty of Israel's God. The more we come to know of science, the more lyrical and majestic the Book of Genesis becomes. This second creation story focuses on the human being. He is made from the dust of the earth but filled with the life and breath of God and placed in a mysterious garden with the tree of the knowledge of good and evil. The last sentence of today's reading gives the story away. Adam personifies each of us before our experience of the power of evil. We all can recall with nostalgia our time in Eden before the conflict of good and evil crashed into our lives. A time bomb is ticking away in Paradise and it is not the serpent. It is Adam's own free will. We cannot live with all our options forever open. Adam would decide, as does every person at some point, where he stood with God.

Gospel Reading

Cleanness and uncleanness are affairs of the soul and not of the body. The Lord tells us that things do not make us evil. The forbidden fruit did not corrupt Eve. It is the disobedience that opens our eyes. If a person has hate in his heart, a thousand Papal blessings will be powerless to help him. If a person is filled with the love of Jesus, a million curses and spells will be harmless. Nothing can separate us from the love of the Lord.

Point

As with Adam, the key to where we stand with God is inside ourselves.

THURSDAY — Fifth Week of the Year
Gn 2:18-25   *Mk 7:24-30*

First Reading

In this ancient account regarding creation, Genesis tells us that Adam could not find an equal among the animals so God constructs a companion, not a slave, from Adam's rib. The rib was chosen by Genesis to explain the deep affinity between man and woman. They are so drawn to one another that they become, in marriage, one flesh. This is a theological vision of the order of things before the onset of sin. Gradually, we will watch this order disintegrate into the world we know. Genesis is actually backtracking from the world as it is to the way it should be. In this early biblical polemic against city life, the family of mankind begins in a garden and not as anonymous strangers warrened in cities.

Gospel Reading

A Gentile woman approaches Jesus for a healing. To this point, the Lord's ministry had been limited to Jewish people: Jairus, the hemorrhaging woman, the crowds of sick in Galilee. He quotes a proverb to her to the effect that charity begins at home — family food is not given to pets. Because she shows the same trust in the Lord as did Jairus and the ailing woman, her daughter is cured. Mark is showing how the in-gathering of both Jews and Gentiles in the early Church began with Jesus' ministry as He restores the bonds among the family of mankind which had been wrecked in that original sin.

Point

The Eucharist is a time to put differences aside and discover each other as brothers and sisters in Christ.

FRIDAY — Fifth Week of the Year
Gn 3:1-8   *Mk 7:31-37*

First Reading

This story of the fall of man and woman contains more than the details of a first and original sin. It is a phenomenology of every sin. The inscape of this first sin explains the contours of all sin. We have all had the experience of losing a piece of our innocence in our first smuggled cigarette, our first clandestine drink, our first infidelity. Our thought processes probably corresponded to those of Eve with a similar result. We realized our nakedness and weakness. This parable of the first sin spotlights the resulting breakdown of the invisible bonds of community that until now had been taken for granted. From this point, people will have to work hard to restore trust among themselves.

Gospel Reading

This brief ceremony used by Jesus signified perhaps a ritualized pattern used by early Christian healers. It expresses His restoration of our ability to again hear God's Word with the same attentiveness we had when we and mankind were young. A great deal has served to obstruct and crowd our hearing in the intervening years. Jesus opens our ears to hear His Word not for instruction but for action; not just for ourselves but for others.

Point

As we learn to hear again the Word of God, we restore our bonds with others.

SATURDAY — Fifth Week of the Year
Gn 3:9-24   Mk 8:1-10

First Reading

All cultures retain some memory of a lost innocence. The results of sin spill out in this first reading as everyone is expelled from the garden. The snake became the crawling reptile we all know. The woman has childbirth pain and will be dominated by her husband. Man will labor to survive and wrest a living from the earth. Sin has disrupted the created order. The companionship of husband and wife became infected with the rhythm of dominance and submission. The raising of children became difficult; earning a living became the burden of one's adult years. Death became a hostile frustration of our ambitions and not a natural conclusion of our life. In the middle of all this appears a hint of coming liberation in the snake's bruising by a human heel. God provides Adam and Eve with clothing to cover their lost innocence in another tiny promise of future restoration.

Gospel Reading

This miracle of the loaves and fish is for the Gentiles. It symbolizes the Eucharist as a new Passover no longer celebrating the Hebrew release from Egypt but the liberation of all mankind from sin. This is the fulfillment of the Genesis promise. The Lord gives us in the Eucharist a way of overcoming the degenerative effects of repeated sin, a vehicle to restore us as sons and daughters of God and a catalyst to regenerate our religious and civil institutions.

Point

Even in our sin, God remains to help us find our way back to the light.

MONDAY — Sixth Week of the Year
Gn 4:1-15, 25 *Mk 8:11-13*

First Reading

The story of Cain and Abel condenses the continuing conflict between the Canaanites and Hebrews, between farmers and shepherds and between brothers. Cain was the first murderer as well as the builder of the first city. In the perspective of Genesis, the founder of civilization was at the same time the father of a long, dark history of fratricide that continues today in the streets of our cities and suburbs. Verses omitted from today's reading quote Lamech, the biblical inventor of the feud, as he recites a hymn to revenge. Sin has a cumulative effect that grows and gels into social structures and mores into which we are born.

Gospel Reading

The Lord castigates a generation that craves signs and wonders. Mark is emphatic that Jesus worked signs as part of His message but did not proclaim Himself a wonderworker. Skepticism and lack of faith can become so institutionalized and so infect an entire generation that the village agnostic becomes a model, a paradigm of universal skepticism with commitment to nothing as an ideal. To such a mentality, Jesus says in effect that He came to heal real pain and to satisfy real spiritual hunger and not idle curiosity.

Point

Sin and grace are never simply personal events.

TUESDAY — Sixth Week of the Year
Gn 6:5-8; 7:1-5, 10   Mk 8:14-21

First Reading

The basis of the story of Noah and the flood was probably a flood that submerged part of Mesopotamia (modern Iraq). It was local but catastrophic and was given universal meaning. Frequently, the ark is pictured as a wooden version of the *Queen Elizabeth II*. Actually, it is described as a tub designed simply to float and not to sail anywhere. After all, there was no place to sail. The ark stands for God's justice and mercy as He preserves a remnant of people to seek a new beginning. As God "puts down His bow," the rainbow reminder is the promise of the constancy of the natural order as well as of the possibility of rebirth in any tragedy. God made a covenant with mankind through Noah. Noah is the biblical inventor of wine, which has its own special history in mankind's affairs. To the early Christians, the ark represented the Church and the flood stood for the waters of Baptism with their cleansing and regenerative power.

Gospel Reading

This reading describes the absence of spiritual sight. The Pharisees wanted a sign but received none. The Apostles received a sign, the miracle of the loaves, but failed to see its meaning. The presence or absence of God is not directly deducible from the presence or absence of wonders. Spiritual sight is still necessary to see God at work. Jesus cautions against the cynicism, or poisoned leaven, of those Pharisees who try to explain everything away by reducing it to political or psychological factors. Neither the source of, nor the solution to, evil in our world is reducible to empirical factors alone.

Point

Spiritual insight enabled the author of Genesis to give everlasting meaning to a regional flood. It enables us to see through bread to the presence of Christ.

WEDNESDAY — Sixth Week of the Year
Gn 8:6, 13, 20-22   Mk 8:22-26

First Reading

The first human artifact after the flood is an altar. God makes a covenant with all creation through Noah with a promise of the recurrence of the seasons. The world's only source of damnation from this point will be mankind and not God. It is a promise of immense hope that God will always provide some instrument for salvation in the middle of the constant turmoils of war and rumors of war. We have an assurance that the few who remain faithful will be God's instruments for universal restoration.

Gospel Reading

The blind man comes to see. This is the only gradual cure in the Gospels and typifies the progressive understanding of the disciples as Jesus becomes more than a teacher for them. It is also a model of our own coming to know and understand the ways of the Lord in our lives. The ability to see through the events of nature and history to an underlying divine purpose and movement does not come in a sudden flash. It is gradual. Our faith assures us that, threaded through the oscillation of pain and pressure in our lives and history, God's design for us and mankind is benign and saving.

Point

Faith grows and matures as we do.

THURSDAY — Sixth Week of the Year
Gn 9:1-13   *Mk 8:27-33*

First Reading

God's covenant with Noah does not return things to the status quo before the flood. Sin is acknowledged as a permanent feature of the human condition. The slaughter and eating of animals is part of this second age of lost innocence. Now, man's dominion over creation will be exercised through force and fear. What in Eden had been expressed in love and presence must now be enforced through covenant and law. Gradually, this covenant with Noah will become more limited, ethnic, and specific until finally in one human being — Who is God — a new covenant will burst open again the bounds of divine life for all people to re-enter.

Gospel Reading

This is the turning point in Mark's Gospel. Jesus, for the first time, describes the great Messiah, whom the Jews had awaited for centuries, as a suffering Messiah. This seemed a contradiction in terms to a Jew. In this brief but crucial passage, Jesus corrects false notions of Messiahship, glory and salvation. He fuses the notion of "Son of Man" as the great eschatological judge in glory with Isaiah's mysterious suffering servant. It will take the rest of the Gospel for this surprise conjunction to penetrate the understanding of the disciples. Mark uses Jesus' words to remind us that our suffering as disciples is not accidental. The avenue of salvific suffering was first traced by Jesus.

The more clearly we follow the Lord, the more will our suffering approximate His. Just as His suffering had the capacity to save and give life, our suffering as disciples has similar power.

Point

The suffering of Jesus will reopen the kingdom to all people.

FRIDAY — Sixth Week of the Year
Gn 11:1-9   *Mk 8:34-9:1*

First Reading

The tower of Babel illustrates the vicious effect of sin on civilization. This event climaxes the entire epic of dislocation that began with Adam and Eve. It brings us into the world as we know it. It shows the effect of pride on human order and life. The result is segregation along racial, national and cultural lines. The fragmentation between Adam and Eve in that original sin increased exponentially to divide the world. With this incident, Genesis has shown by parable and example how far into suspicion and division the world had fallen after its creation by a good God. It was not God who brought evil into our world. That was mankind's special contribution.

Gospel Reading

This is not an isolated saying of Jesus on commitment. He asks us to dedicate ourselves completely to the Father's kingdom. The mood shifts not only to a discussion of the suffering Messiah but to a discussion of the suffering His disciples must expect in their own lives. In a society distorted by sin, arrogance and greed, it will be systemically difficult to follow the

Lord. The Jesus we meet in Mark's Gospel presents a message that is severe and powerful. If we are to follow Him in His suffering, we are assured that His glory will be ours as well. Discipleship is a composite of pain and the promise of transcendent glory.

Point

Suffering is a fact of life which Jesus made into a virtue of the spiritual life.

SATURDAY — Sixth Week of the Year
Heb 11:1-7   *Mk 9:2-13*

First Reading

Our reflection on the first chapters of Genesis concludes with an exhortation to faith written after Jesus' Resurrection. The Letter to the Hebrews speaks of the faith of the patriarchs. It was a faith that did not inherit centuries of theological tradition and religious culture. In retrospect, we can see their heroism profiled against the brutality of the times. The faith of the patriarchs, primitive and undifferentiated by our standards, was new and dynamic amid the pagan milieu of the bronze age. The writer of the Letter to the Hebrews encourages us to keep faith in a world hostile in different ways to the deepest yearnings of faith.

Gospel Reading

In a moment of glory, on a mountain called Tabor, disciples whose faith had been shaken by Jesus' prediction of approaching death are lifted up as they glimpse Him in His majesty. In the figures of Moses and Elijah they came to see that

Jesus indeed embodied all the promise, hope and fidelity that rushed throughout the Old Testament story. Jesus tells them that Elijah — singleminded in his covenant devotion, taken to heaven in a chariot of fire and rumored in Jewish legend to return to announce the coming Messiah — has indeed come back in the person of John the Baptist. In this vision soaked with the majesty and power of God we are reminded that this glory is destined for us as well. But as with Jesus, a cross will precede the glory.

Point

Suffering reveals our dignity and glory. It unlocks the deepest part of ourselves.

MONDAY — Seventh Week of the Year
Si1:1-10   *Mk 9:14-29*

First Reading

Today, we begin an Old Testament book written by a man called Ben-Sirach. Sometimes called *Ecclesiasticus,* the "Book of the Church," it is a meditation on wisdom written two centuries before Christ for Jews living in a Greek culture. Wisdom here can mean know-how in the business of living through an appreciation of the fit of individual events into a larger scheme of things. Wisdom can also mean the plan of God as experienced in creation. The ability to live our life thoughtfully and harmoniously with others according to God's plan is a skill.

The composition of wisdom sayings was an international commonplace that grew out of local folkways and communities. This tradition was not static but grew over the years into the various strands of what we have come to call the wisdom literature. Sirach writes toward the end of this tradition and identifies wisdom with the observance of Torah Law. For Sirach, the Torah Law is revealed wisdom. In today's reading he reminds us that wisdom is a gift from God. Divine wisdom cannot easily be read out of a book or memorized in school even though Sirach himself seems to have run something like a wisdom academy. His point is that wisdom is more important than analytical knowledge because it enables us to see a core of principle embedded in the hundreds of situations we meet every day.

Gospel Reading

In this incident of the impotence of the disciples to effect a cure, we are reminded that there are dysfunctions in the moral life of others and of ourselves that no amount of human skill can cure and for which we need the power of the Lord. This reading highlights the need of the Church and of church people to recognize that our power comes from the Lord and not simply from human wisdom. Jesus has given the Gospel saving power. Profound human transformation is not simply an intellectual or emotional affair. It is the power of Christ making us a new creation.

Point

Wisdom enables us to integrate our lives through common sense. Divine wisdom enables us to integrate our common sense through faith.

TUESDAY — Seventh Week of the Year
Si 2:1-11   *Mk 9:30-37*

First Reading

Sirach describes our obligations to God. Serving the Lord

has its share of trials deriving from the clash of our expectations with the plan of God or from our search for an immediate type of success. These testings purify and strengthen our trust in God. An overarching design of God is threaded through the lives of individuals as well as the affairs of nations. Wisdom looks beyond the immediate frame of reference toward that design and rationale. Sirach reminds us that God can draw out new spiritual vitality from what appear to be short-term defeats.

Gospel Reading

This is Jesus' second prediction of His coming suffering, death and Resurrection. He continues to explain to the disciples not the specifics of the Resurrection glory but the necessity of the pain and suffering preceding it. This is the question that plagues every Christian heart and mind. In another instance of the kingdom's reversal of our culture's values, the Lord reminds us that true human greatness lies in service to others. This is a majesty of the human spirit that will become apparent for all to appreciate on the last day.

Point

God can draw life from apparent death.

WEDNESDAY — Seventh Week of the Year
Si 4:11-19   *Mk 9:38-40*

First Reading

Wisdom is portrayed here as an independent entity and is personified as a nourishing mother. Sirach describes the benefits she brings to those who cherish her. We cannot own wisdom as we do a car. The precondition for living wisely is to live according to our traditions which embody the accumulated wisdom of generations. These traditions express a way of looking at the world. Wisdom is not composed of bullets of information or a string of *bon mots* disconnected from the rest of life. It is a way of living our life. The last verse makes the point: if we fail her, she will abandon us. There is an order that undergirds the seeming chaos of human life. That order is not simply the result of a subjective imposition or cultural style. It is a profoundly moral order accessible to human intelligence that we disregard at our own long-range risk.

Gospel Reading

Jesus reminds His small community of disciples of the good will that exists in the world. In the Old Testament, wisdom was not confined to Judaism but was perceived to extend throughout the community of nations. Nobody has a lock on wisdom. In Jesus, that wisdom of God became flesh and blood. Conclusions about the purpose of life upon which different cultures had variously hit were given the clear and forceful expression of a revelation by the teaching and cross of Christ. Nevertheless, people who do not carry the name "Christian" attempt to live deeply moral lives. The grace of Christ is not completely absent from their hearts. What is critical is not the title we carry but the results we achieve.

Point

The moral order that pervades human life is perceptible to all people.

THURSDAY — Seventh Week of the Year
Si 5:1-8   *Mk 9:41-50*

First Reading

Sirach warns against the illusory security that attends our

placing trust in the wrong things. Financial success or physical beauty are not automatic insurers of happiness. The religious face of this false security is called presumption. A person should not feel free to sin in the expectation of God's repeated forgiveness because that forgiveness is predicated on a serious purpose of amendment. If the wise man does not idolize material success, neither does he tinker with his spiritual life.

It is not the things we have but how we use them that creates an ordered life.

Gospel Reading

The Lord encourages us to rid ourselves of those things that encumber spiritual growth. The difficult but fulfilled venture we call discipleship is exemplified in the saints. Jesus' three sayings about salt are enigmatic, originally independent and loosely connected here. We can apply them, however to our discipleship. (1) The fire (salt) of difficulty will test and shape each disciple's commitment. (2) If we disciples lose our special sense of mission (salt) in the world, society itself cannot restore it. (3) As we disciples become increasingly conscious of the Holy Spirit within us (salt) we will become an articulate, bold community of faith on the offense and no longer be only defensive.

Point

The goals we seek influence the kind of life we live.

FRIDAY — Seventh Week of the Year
Si 6:5-17 *Mk 10:1-12*

First Reading

Water seeks its own level. We get the friends that we deserve. These two pieces of universal wisdom constitute the thrust of today's selection from Sirach. He reminds us to be discerning in our choice of close friends. He dwells on the subject of friendship more than any other biblical writer, possibly reflecting a fund of bitter experience. We may not have a great deal of freedom in our choice of associates and co-workers, but the people with whom we share our deepest feelings and hopes are very much within our choice. He tells us to beware of fair-weather friends in particular. Because we bump into all kinds of people, Sirach advises caution. Wisdom extends not only to our own internal self but also to the social world that we slowly build around ourselves over a lifetime.

Gospel Reading

Jesus speaks about fidelity in marriage. Marriage is the premier example of the importance of wisdom in the choice of friends. For a huge number of reasons, divorce is a fact of everyday Catholic life. Although analyses of this phenomenon abound, the pastoral responsibility of the parish to the divorced is clear. A support system of friends for those who are experiencing such a trauma is very important. No community that carries the name Christian can throw its wounded overboard. If the Church has been given any clear mission from the Lord, it is to continue His ministry of healing.

Point

Wisdom not only governs our choice of friends; it also enables us to be an effective friend to others.

SATURDAY — Seventh Week of the Year
Si 17:1-15   *Mk 10:13-16*

First Reading

This extended reflection on the glory and potential of

human beings is really a meditative blend of tradition and interpretation on the first chapters of Genesis. Sirach describes the great power and promise that belong to us as images of God. The basic reason for the emergence of wisdom literature in the first place is the fact that we do have a measure of control over the conduct of our lives. Unlike the animal world, we are not locked into instinctual routines. Our intellectual and moral equipment enable us to craft our lives skillfully. This is a great gift that can easily be abused by turning from God's purpose for us and the manifold ways that we might fulfill it. God has endowed us with a share of His intelligence and creativity to fashion a life which continues His creative design.

Gospel Reading

The point of our accepting the reign of God as little children is not naive innocence but wholehearted acceptance. Wisdom is not naive. Sirach wrote after the many years of tribulation which the Jewish people endured. Yet, he could speak about the importance of faith in God. The Genesis meditation beats with a lively and experienced faith. It is the same kind of total trust to which Jesus is calling us.

Point

The act of faith is unique to human beings, as is also the fact of sin.

MONDAY — Eighth Week of the Year
Si 17:19-27   *Mk 10:17-27*

First Reading

Sirach was giving expression to the worldview of Judaism much as Luigi Barzini writes about "The Italians" and "The Europeans." In Sirach we see the world as Jews saw it very close to the time of Jesus. Some claim, in fact, that Sirach's outlook is similar to that of those who will come to be known as Sadducees. The theme of this first reading is repentance as a way back to God. There is a dynamic to the spiritual life. There are many ways to describe it. The upward spiral of repentance and forgiveness is one model. Sirach underscores the urgency of repentance as a luxury of the living. When our life comes to a close the chance to change finishes as well. As an embryonic Sadducee, Sirach had no articulate view of the next life. However, his message of repentance remains valid for us.

Gospel Reading

Jesus speaks to a wealthy man about communion with God on a level deeper than he had known. He challenges him to go beyond the avoidance of evil. Specifically, the Lord directs him to give up his wealth. Each of us has his or her own block to further spiritual growth. It may be power, position, certain social contacts, a particular circle of friends or special pastimes. It will differ for each individual. Furthermore, these obstacles are dynamic. They change, grow and transmute. In the same way, Christian perfection is not a state but a process as we try to let the healing power of the Holy Spirit penetrate more deeply into our selves. By trying to do so, we follow a path travelled by centuries of Christian pilgrims seeking deeper communion with God.

Point

Sin and grace are both dynamic. They carry their own momentum toward or away from God.

TUESDAY — Eighth Week of the Year
Si 35:1-12   *Mk 10:28-31*

First Reading

Sirach reviews various Old Testament rituals: the oblation, peace offering, alms and cereal offering from the Temple liturgy. He concludes that a good life is worth more than all of these. Liturgical preoccupation is a great deal easier than covenant living. This is a favorite Old Testament prophetic theme. It is less a rejection of liturgy and ceremony as prayer than it is a rejection of liturgy and ceremony as a substitute for covenant living. A fervently recited novena cannot replace the effort to keep peace with our neighbor. Sirach's teaching here is that religious practices have value to the extent that they give liturgical expression to what is actually transpiring in the rest of our lives. Otherwise, liturgy becomes an elaborate attempt at ceremonial bribery.

Gospel Reading

If Sirach describes empty gestures, the Gospel reading goes a step further to show that good intentions are not sufficient. They have value when we try to give them concrete expression in our lives. If basic Christian living presents no formidable challenge to us, then perhaps Jesus is calling us to a more intense form of discipleship. Perhaps He is calling us to simplify our life style, engage in a more active prayer life, a more demonstrative parish involvement or to expend ourselves in wider service to an individual in need. To compensate for everything we give to His service, the Lord promises a qualitatively greater reward not only in this life but in the next as well.

Point

Correct ritual alone or good intentions alone are incomplete. Both must be validated by how we live our life.

WEDNESDAY — Eighth Week of the Year
Si 36:1, 5-6, 10-17   *Mk 10:32-45*

First Reading

This messianic prayer for God to show His power and bring glory to His people belongs to the faithful of every age. We might examine what form such glory would take. Are God's people glorified by financial success, political clout, deference from other religions, the ability to control others? The Lord has told and shown us that the real glory of human beings comes not in the exercise of raw animal power over each other, but in service and in helping our fellow human beings. The glory of God's people comes in our service to the rest of mankind.

Gospel Reading

As the disciples get caught up in the anticipation of a utopian kingdom, Jesus brings them back to the real world as He speaks for the third time about the suffering to come. He reminds them again that true glory is found in service. We can ask Sirach's question of the Church. What is the measure of the Church's success? Is it plant size, numbers, organizational efficiency, total theological harmony? Or is it the Gospel preached with vigor; a place of community in a mobile age; a place where values are cherished in an ethically agnostic society; a place to be brothers and sisters in a career-crazed culture; a place where the Lord Jesus lives, speaks and loves? Perhaps the Church is at its best as a minority, a leaven, a light, a little flock. The Church's moment of glory has never been when it played the games of high politics or high finance.

We can ask ourselves as well what the sign of personal holiness might be: visions, stigmata, the gift of tears, the odor of sanctity, tongue-speaking or service to others.

Point

The measure of success for ourselves and for the Church is not how many people serve us but how many we can serve.

THURSDAY — Eighth Week of the Year
Si 42:15-25   *Mk 10:46-52*

First Reading

This first reading is a lyric in praise of the Creator God's wisdom reflected in the structure of nature. For many people who do not have access to the Scriptures or for whom its words no longer speak with power, there is the magnificence of creation in which to discover the splendor of God. More thrilling than the glory of the universe is the power found deep within the human heart. It is the human being's ability to love, create and forgive that reflects the wisdom of God most vividly. The universe moves along its appointed course. But the wisdom of God is given fresh, dramatic and unprecedented expression with the birth of each new baby. We are vessels of God's wisdom.

Gospel Reading

Blind Bartimaeus represents many things, one of which is the vision of faith. The biblical/Christian vision of the world does not see everything in exclusively biblical terms. It does not use biblical language to exclude science and our broader cultural surrounding from its mind. It does not turn from the world to gaze exclusively at the pages of a Bible. But it does use the Scriptures to find a way of looking at the world. It sees God at work in human history and in the human spirit. It sees a world "charged with the grandeur of God." The Christian vision is one of hope. It sees beyond darkness to light, beyond sin to forgiveness and beyond death to life.

Point

The Christian does not see different things from the rest of society. He or she sees the same things in a different way — in the light of Christ.

FRIDAY — Eighth Week of the Year
Si 44:1, 9-13   *Mk 11:11-26*

First Reading

Sirach praises godly men (and women) loyal to the covenant: kings, governors, musicians — an entire galaxy of stars. His purpose is to show the fruitfulness of faith in the effect and memory these holy ones left behind. There is no clear notion of personal immortality in Sirach. The immortality he describes is that of a good reputation that outlives its bearer. There are many others, unknown to us, who were godly people as well and whose goodness lives on in the effects they had on their families and others. How vast the number of such people really is will always remain unknown. Planes that land do not make the newspapers. These holy people do not receive the press coverage that is given to assassins and tyrants. We should not be deceived by the amount of copy given to evil. The number of just and godly individuals is far more extensive and pervasive throughout history.

Gospel Reading

It is important to see this incident of the fig tree in the larger context which the New English Bible labels as "the final challenge to Jerusalem.'' The events of these chapters of Mark occur in the twilight of Old Testament Judaism. The Lord's judgment on the fig tree is a dramatic act symbolizing the fate of institutional Judaism. This is not a judgment on the spirit of those holy ones who kept the covenant spirit in their lives. That remnant will constitute the beginning of the New Israel. These anawim, unlike the Pharisees at the top of the social ladder, were the carriers of the faith of Abraham and Moses into the new age begun by Jesus.

Point

The good (and evil) we do has a multiplier effect. We can never predict the full extent of its reach.

SATURDAY — Eighth Week of the Year
Si 51:12-20   *Mk 11:27-33*

First Reading

We come to the end of Sirach. He describes the pursuit of wisdom as being like a groom's chase of a bride. We all would like to attain that sense of balance and equanimity that enables us to respond to the events of our life in a proportionate way. If we could ever attain such a state, we would not be easily disoriented by a sudden change of circumstance or tragedy in our life. In the Old Testament, wisdom is not an exclusively religious concept. In the New Testament, it is described as a gift of the Holy Spirit. In either case, we are raised above the immediacy of events to a more sweeping view of life and God's design. Such a gift precludes our questioning God's love for us when our car will not start on a cold winter morning. Wisdom allows us to see the larger picture.

Gospel Reading

We see a model of wisdom in action in Jesus' ministry. It is fascinating to catalogue the variety of responses Jesus gave to the different people who crossed His path. He shows us a very diverse and many-sided ministry. We can compare the challenge Jesus hurls at the cynical elders in today's Gospel reading with His inviting response to the woman at the well, His gentle encouragement of Nicodemus, His rebuke and forgiveness of Peter as well as His response to the centurion, Bartimaeus, the children, Jairus and the widow of Naim. Jesus' brief ministry is a rich treasure of diverse pastoral styles directed always toward individuals and their special needs. It is wisdom in action.

Point

Living the Christian life is a skill. It comes with practice and the Holy Spirit.

MONDAY — Ninth Week of the Year
Tb 1:1-2;2:1-9   *Mk 12:1-12*

First Reading

The story of Tobit is a docudrama of wisdom in action. In this popular romance, Tobit and his son represent the Jewish people during the exile faced with the very real danger of an uncritical and ultimately suicidal amalgamation of their faith with the surrounding non-Jewish culture. The story is constructed to exhibit what faith in the God of Israel looks like in a non-Israelite setting when God seems to have abandoned His people. A part of the sophisticated message of this book is that Israel survives as an attitude and approach to God and is not confined to the geographical boundaries of the Holy Land. Tobit is the man of faith, true to his traditions. As we enter the story, he had been previously fired by the king for following the Jewish practice of burying the dead within a set period of time. In today's reading, Tobit does it again. He is as fearless in his loyalty to tradition as he is careless about his career.

Gospel Reading

In these final sections of Mark's Gospel, Jesus laments the infidelity of the Jewish people symbolized in the tenants' refusal to respect the agents and son of the king. The gutting of Jerusalem years later scarred the Jewish soul and colored the early Christian interpretation of this parable. The fidelity of Tobit to tradition can be contrasted to the fidelity of the Jerusalem elite less to tradition than to conventional religious arrangements that proved comfortable and profitable for them. The Lord never indicts the ancient tradition of the Old Testament Torah Law. Instead, He questions the quasi-sacred status accorded a variety of conventional behaviors that had, over time, supplanted the covenant faith. This was Jerusalem's faithlessness.

Point

Tradition is sacred; conventions are important but not sacred.

TUESDAY — Ninth Week of the Year
Tb 2:9-14   *Mk 12:13-17*

First Reading

Tobit has just completed a sacred burial obligation at great personal risk when, during the night, a freak accident occurs. He is blinded by bird droppings — a ridiculous quirk of fate to a man of such deep faith. Because of his incapacity, his wife enters the work force, does remarkably well and returns one day with a bonus goat for her work. Tobit refuses to believe it to be a gift and an argument ensues in which the frustration that had built up within his wife explodes into an accusation of his naivete. The story is told this way to point to a basic truth of human life. In Tobit's case as well as that of the world at large, there is no immediate and universal connection between virtue and worldly success. The reward of a holy life is on a deeper and more enduring level.

Gospel Reading

Mark portrays a mounting tension between Jesus and the religious teachers in these final days. The issue of taxes was a hot one among the Jews. It was one phase of a cluster of burning questions concerning autonomy, emperor worship and Jewish identity. Jesus' reply assures them, in effect, that the power of Rome is insignificant compared to the force of God's kingdom. Such tribute to Caesar is not a fatal concession by the Church because Church and State are not, in this case, equal competitors. The early Church understood the Lord's words to mean that there is no intrinsic opposition between our civic responsibilities and our religious obligations. Disagreement with public policies incompatible with Christian belief and practice is itself an expression of our citizenship in two worlds. Our faith requires that we be responsible citizens.

Point

How we serve the State is a way of witnessing to the kingdom.

WEDNESDAY — Ninth Week of the Year
Tb 3:1-11, 16   *Mk 12:18-27*

First Reading

Both the blinded Tobit and Sarah, a hapless bride, pour out their laments to God. Geographically, they are miles apart from each other. Their misfortunes, however, make them closer in spirit than Tobit is to his wife or than Sarah is to her servants. There are deep bonds of suffering that link people around the world to each other. In the face of cancer, for example, political affiliation and national origin sink into insignificance. People whose paths would never otherwise cross discover in a hospital that the commonality of our humanity is far deeper than the differences we so frequently create and celebrate. Suffering is a common denominator of all people. Tobit and Sarah's prayers end at the same time and with the same trust in God. Raphael is sent to heal them not only in body but in spirit as well.

Gospel Reading

The Sadducees were a priestly elite. They recounted this bizarre story of a bride and seven brothers to ridicule the notion of individual resurrection. Their case was an instance of a Levirate marriage. If a brother died childless, the next brother would marry the widow and the resulting child was deemed to be that of the deceased brother. In response, Jesus explains that the mystery of eternal life is not a projection of this life. We can only approach the mysteries of our faith through metaphors, symbols and images. Such images should not be forced to carry a load for which they were not built. They are not to be taken literally. Rather, they are pointers which stretch our minds beyond the present into the mystery of God. Of course, we need faith to be able to go beyond images. That was a point the Sadducees never reached.

Point

Humility before the mystery of God enables us to keep theologies in perspective.

THURSDAY — Ninth Week of the Year
Tb 6:11; 7:1, 9-14; 8:4-7   *Mk 12:13-17*

First Reading

Tobiah proceeds to collect a debt owed to his father Tobit. He sees the beautiful Sarah and his companion Raphael becomes a marriage broker. Her father, Raguel, agrees to the marriage but feels that there is something that Tobiah should know. He tells him that the previous seven husbands who married Sarah all dropped dead on their wedding night. Tobiah is undaunted but understandably apprehensive. As they go to bed, he suggests that he and Sarah pray as they never prayed before. Their prayer reflects the moving theology of marriage in late Judaism which was part of Jesus' heritage. Also, marriage is not primarily based here on romantic attraction as much as on the good of the Jewish people. If Sarah had not married a fellow-Jew, her property would have been transferred to Gentiles. Community good took precedence over individual good. This marriage of Sarah and Tobiah is seen here as another providential, albeit small, step in God's preservation of His chosen people. Purity of heart and not magic incantations will conquer the demon that persecuted Sarah. Tobiah greets the next morning as Sarah's new husband — alive and well!

Gospel Reading

This is the last of the controversies in these final days. After the questions of taxes and individual resurrection, there comes the issue of the greatest commandment. Jesus responds that love of God and of neighbor are conjoined. He describes not a magic formula or catechism answer but a way of life. For some people, such a response is too unfocused and insufficiently specific. The Lord tells us that we must constantly balance and rebalance the tension between love of God and of neighbor. Over time, we will inevitably overemphasize one over the other. It is the constant effort to keep the balance together, especially with the realization that there is a balance to be kept, that provides the creative energy of Christian growth.

Point

There is no magic formula that absolves us from constantly examining the balance of God and neighbor in our lives.

FRIDAY — Ninth Week of the Year
Tb 11:5-15   *Mk 12:35-37*

First Reading

In this touching homecoming scene, the blind Tobit is healed and gives thanks. The tragedy of his blindness enabled him to appreciate the gift of sight. The lesson from Tobit's tragedy which the book draws is not that people of faith afflicted with blindness will receive their physical sight as quickly as did Tobit. The deeper point is that faith can turn tragedy into a moment of insight. We need not be hapless victims of suffering. We can turn our pain into a vehicle of holiness just as pressure can transmute coal into a diamond. The facts of life and death are neutral. We give them positive or negative meaning by our response to them. The Book of Tobit points to Tobit's faith that gave him deeper insight into himself and into God despite his blindness.

Gospel Reading

At the very end of Jesus' public ministry, He resumes the role of teacher. The controversies are behind Him. He uses a style of rabbinic argument to illuminate the title of "Son of David." There were many sons of David because the Davidic line had by no means been exhausted. After all, Joseph had been of the house and family of David. The Lord is saying that the Son of David who was the object of messianic expectation would be more than a genetic heir of David. He would be a Son of God as well. Davidic descent is secondary. What is distinct about the promised Messiah is His perfect obedience to the Father in heaven. This submission to God's will would be the mark of the Messiah and of His people.

Point

Through faith, we can endow events over which we have no control with saving meaning. Obedience to the Father can turn any tragedy into a Resurrection event.

SATURDAY — Ninth Week of the Year
Tb 12:1, 5-15, 20   *Mk 12:38-44*

First Reading

Raphael finally reveals that he is an angelic agent of God. In his discourse, he sounds very much like a wisdom writer with a Deuteronomic twist. He tells Tobit and his family that the good life of prayer and almsgiving is the greatest worship one can give to God. Of course, Jewish people in exile were far removed from the Temple and could not participate in its services. They came to see that tradition, righteous living and the study of the Torah Law were the best expressions of covenant living. Raphael expresses this anti-legalist viewpoint with the statement that a few alms given with righteousness are better than a fortune poured from a wicked heart. Tobit and his family remind us that there was a great deal more to Judaism around the time of Jesus than the Pharisees as presented in the Gospels. There was the stream of faithful covenant-people from which would come the family of Jesus as well as the first disciples.

Gospel Reading

Raphael's statement is the link with today's Gospel reading. Jesus warns His disciples about the ostentatious piety of the scribes. In a scene heavy with irony, the hope of Israel is embodied in a poor widow who places the few pennies she has into a poor box. With a single gesture, this unknown woman captured the heart of the message of the classic prophets, the wisdom writings and Jesus' teaching about the Law. Here, in the middle of the highly politicized city of Jerusalem, the center of hostility to Jesus, comes a woman at the very end of Jesus' ministry who stands for the best and richest spirituality which the Old Testament and Jerusalem have to offer. She represents everything Israel could have been.

Point

The great triumphs of the Holy Spirit occur within the human heart.

MONDAY — Tenth Week of the Year
2 Cor 1:1-7   *Mt 5:1-12*

First Reading

Our text of Paul's Second Letter to the Corinthians is actually a composite of three different letters. The conflicts within the Corinthian Church were persistent and deep. Paul had received news that some partial reconciliation had occurred between himself and the Corinthian Church as well as among its members. In addressing both his own suffering and that of the Corinthians, Paul tells us in this first reading not to be acquiescent victims, easily rolled over by difficulties. He suggests that we actively use our painful experiences and the comfort we have received from Christ as an apostolate to others. Personal pain teaches us compassion and helps us to realize the deep bonds of brotherhood, sisterhood and creaturehood that connect us to each other and to God.

Gospel Reading

The Sermon on the Mount, Matthew's anthology of Jesus' collected sayings, commences with the Beatitudes. Our English version has attained virtually sacral status similar to the translation of the Lord's Prayer which no translator dare dislodge. Vast homiletic energy is, therefore, poured into explaining the modern equivalents of these hallowed phrases. "Poor in spirit" — those receptive to the presence of God will experience the kingdom. "Sorrowing" — those who appreciate the depth of evil in the world will see the triumph of God. "Meek" — those with self-control know what true dominion is. . . . These Beatitudes resonate with the spirituality of the Old Testament and hurl a paradox through the middle of our complacency. In the very things which conventional wisdom tells us to avoid, we can most fully experience God and His reign. Everything that our culture considers valuable cannot provide that deep vulnerability that makes us open to the action of God.

Point

We come to know God not only in vaulting cathedrals but in the ordinary and seemingly disappointing moments of our lives as well.

TUESDAY — Tenth Week of the Year
2 Cor 1:18-22   *Mt 5:13-16*

First Reading

It is difficult, at first, to plug into Paul's problem in this first reading. Evidently, his opponents were charging that his vacillation in regard to the time of a projected visit was symptomatic of more serious doctrinal inconsistencies on his part. His unreliability in the simple keeping of appointments reflected unfavorably on his teaching. Paul retorts that he had never spoken from both sides of his mouth. His Gospel and he are as trustworthy as the Lord Jesus Himself.

What people know initially of Christ is what they see in Christians.

Gospel Reading

Jesus speaks of salt and light. The disciples are to be salt and light not only for the revival of Judaism but of the world. If we refuse to be the salt and light of the earth, our faith can easily become vulgarized into harmless chocolate images of Christ and religious scenes painted on dinner plates — the harmless artifacts of a faith with all the backbone of a seedless grape. If Catholics have the same crime and divorce rates as everyone else, perhaps we are losing our power to witness. In a culture as aggressively proselytic as ours, we can easily fall into the trap of assimilating popular cultural values while retaining the semblance of Christian identity only in vocabulary and ceremony. The Christians who have most deeply impressed us are generally not those who lead crusades. It is the incidental assist at a roadside or supermarket that leaves a powerfully memorable witness.

Point

Like salt and light, our faith is most operative when it is part of the everyday texture of our lives.

WEDNESDAY — Tenth Week of the Year
2 Cor 3:4-11   *Mt 5:17-19*

First Reading

Paul calls the Law a "ministry of death." This phrase can be easily misunderstood. He is not opposing old and new covenants as though the old covenant suddenly became evil and inoperative. What had been reverenced for generations as God's gift to the Jewish people did not suddenly become junk. That is not what Paul is asserting nor what the early Church believed. Paul contrasts the uses made of the Law. The written Law alone can kill while the spirit of that Law gives life.

Gospel Reading

While Matthew's Gospel is steeped in the Jewish tradition, it is also a sharp critique of the standardizing Pharisaic approach to the tradition. The first disciples had been accused of violating Sabbath fasting and ritual requirements. Matthew wrote his Gospel for Jewish Christians excluded from the synagogue during a period of Jewish doctrinal retrenchment after the destruction of Jerusalem, to show how Jesus indeed fulfills the heart of the Torah Law. The Lord states in this first reading that He came not to abolish but to complete the Law much as a grown plant draws out the power resident in the seed. "Law" and "Spirit" do not represent conflicting testaments or religions. They are two ways of approaching God. With "Law" the approach to God and the spiritual life is legal; salvation is juridical. Legal fulfillment is identified with spiritual fulfillment. "Spirit" locates salvation in our personal link with the Lord and others, of which Law and tradition are important but partial expressions. Law and tradition focus and structure our spiritual life as a prism focuses light. But the prism is not the light. Law and tradition do not save. They are vehicles for the concrete expression of a supernatural, sanctifying relationship with the Lord.

Point

Exact legal compliance is no substitute for the saving knowledge of Jesus Christ.

THURSDAY — Tenth Week of the Year
2 Cor 3:15-4:1, 3-6   *Mt 5:20-26*

First Reading

Paul speaks of a veil that covers the Jewish mind when Moses (the Torah Law) is read. Only when they turn to the Lord will the veil be removed. In the light of Christ, the Old Testament words and experience acquire deeper meaning. In the Old Testament, we see savagery, butchery, sexual excess, call, law, covenant, a growing sense of peoplehood, prophetic reminders of covenant living — in short, a process of gradual transformation from children of Adam to a people of God. The entire biblical record, even at its most brutal, exhibits God's reconciliation of people to Himself. The final catalyst of this journey is Jesus through whom we receive the transforming power of grace deep in our heart.

Gospel Reading

Jesus tells us that holiness is not simply compliance with a legal code but personal transformation. He fleshes this out through a set of six examples to show that the Law of Moses did not go far enough toward internal change.

It is important not simply to avoid murder but to evict from within us the brooding anger that makes us want to commit murder. Our spiritual life is not hermetically sealed from our emotional life. The understanding of an individual harboring a grudge at this very moment, for example, would be veiled as they hear this very Gospel reading. Our anger and jealousy, however deeply we think we may have buried them within us, cloud our comprehension of the Gospel message and block the action of God's Spirit. On the other hand, our aggressive search for reconciliation can uncover new levels of meaning in the Gospel message.

Point

Reconciliation with others releases our spiritual vitality.

FRIDAY — Tenth Week of the Year
2 Cor 4:7-15   Mt 5:27-32

First Reading

We have a soaring reflection by Paul on the life of an apostle and of any Christian. We are frail creatures who carry inside us the indestructible glory and power of God. As a result, although we endure failures and problems as does everyone else, we are not destroyed by them because the same power that raised Jesus from the grave lives in us. There is a further point. Our suffering as Christians does not imply that we have failed or that our faith is a mirage. We suffer as the followers of Jesus because He suffered. The daily deaths and risings we experience trace the passion and Resurrection of the Lord into our own life. This very tracing of Jesus' paschal mystery in our lives plants it into our own time and neighborhood.

Gospel Reading

Jesus continues to strike at the roots of sin located not primarily in conduct but in the impulses that drive and feed our behavior. Certainly there are thoughts and feelings whose source is beyond our control. The feelings, suggestions and fantasies that we do foster and allow to congregate on the street corners of our minds can be as destructive of a marriage relationship as any overt infidelity. We cannot say that our private thoughts are harmless because they hurt nobody. They sap our dedication, love and singlemindedness toward others. Doing battle with our darker impulses can be more arduous (and more spiritually productive) than a medieval crusade.

Point

We can experience the passion of Christ not only through external pressure but also through dying to ourselves.

SATURDAY — Tenth Week of the Year
2 Cor 5:14-21   *Mt 5:33-37*

First Reading

Paul reveals the driving force behind his apostolic work to be the love of Jesus for us. Jesus changed mankind. In His death, the suicidal streak we inherited from Adam was nailed to the cross and killed. In Jesus' Resurrection, a new source of life entered the human story. Whether we Christians recognize it or not, we are a fresh creation. Our past has become irrelevant in God's sight. Every part of us has been made new in Christ. Paul's theological assertion of total qualitative change emerged from his own experience of transformation, forgiveness and gifted love on the Damascus road. That single event so colored his entire theology that he made himself the reporter of this remarkable power and gift to all mankind. In the same way, we announce this message of new life with a conviction in direct proportion to our experience of it.

Gospel Reading

Religious oaths are Jesus' subject in this portion of the Sermon on the Mount. He condemns the use of oaths and religious language for self-centered, manipulative and evasive purposes. The abuse toward which He points is far wider than fake oaths. It is found in a casuistry that retains the vocabulary of faith while sucking out its substance. The Lord refers to religious doubletalk which sounds solemn and elevating but says nothing. Where we stand and what we believe should be clear as crystal to those who deal with us.

Point

If we are a new creation, that change should be evidenced in our conversation, clothing, homes and use of leisure time. We cannot be a "new creation" part-time.

MONDAY — Eleventh Week of the Year
2 Cor 6:1-10   Mt 5:38-42

First Reading

Paul justifies his claim of apostolic authority by drawing the Corinthians' attention to a striking paradox. Although he has been the object of a string of humiliations, physical abuses and disinformation campaigns, the Gospel and the power of God are still conveyed to others through him. The same is true of ourselves. With all the limitations and failures that clutter our lives, we still carry within us the image of Christ and the power of the Holy Spirit from our baptism. However obscured that image and power may have become over the years, they remain the seeds of spiritual revival planted deep inside us.

Gospel Reading

The Old Testament saying, "A tooth for a tooth" (Lv 24:19; Ex 21:22), was not the endorsement of revenge it is popularly interpreted to be. Its purpose was to cap conflict. If someone knocked out one of your teeth, for example, you were not justified in knocking out all of his: just a tooth for a tooth — nothing more! Although money damages were probably the usual custom, the rule was given graphic statement to limit the violence that fuels the cycle of reaction.

Jesus spells out the deep purpose behind this biblical injunction by telling us not simply to avoid retaliation but to forgive. Forgiveness is the only way to interrupt the endless and destructive recycling of hatred and revenge.

Point

How we deal with conflicts that lace our daily life depends upon how vividly the image of Jesus shines in our life.

TUESDAY — Eleventh Week of the Year
2 Cor 8:1-9   *Mt 5:43-48*

First Reading

Our money and our enemies are two subjects that serve as stress tests for Christians. In today's first reading, Paul is asking for money as he takes up a collection for the nearly bankrupt Jerusalem Church. He points to the example of the Macedonian Christians who showed phenomenal generosity despite their own financial problems. He appoints Titus to collect the money. Our financial contribution to the Church is not isolated from the rest of our spiritual life. It deserves prayerful thought because it is one tangible demonstration of our faith. The money we share with the parish is a measure of how serious we are about our Catholicism.

Gospel Reading

A second stress test appears in the Gospel reading. Some people have an uncanny ability to bring out the worst in us. They seem to tap levels of antipathy deep within us whose depth we never quite appreciated before. The test is not how we treat people who share our wave-length but how we deal with those who are on a completely different frequency. Adult love is not measured by the character of those with whom we come into contact. The love of which the Lord speaks is neither romantic nor emotional. It is a recognition of the same kind of responsibility to our fellow-Christians as we have to a fractious relative. It is a clear-headed judgment that beneath our differences we are linked together in the Lord.

Point

How we handle money and enemies stretches our spiritual muscles. Holiness is not a state but a process.

WEDNESDAY — Eleventh Week of the Year
2 Cor 9:6-11   *Mt 6:1-6, 16-18*

First Reading

Paul writes further about the collection for the Jerusalem Church. His quotation from the Old Testament book of Sirach that "God loves a cheerful giver" probably had the same effect among the Corinthians that it has in any parish today.

Our act of placing money in a collection basket means several things. It acknowledges that our wealth is a gift and not something to be hoarded; it symbolizes the work we do; it enables us to share in the mission of the local and of the international Church; it demonstrates our faith in God's continuing generosity to us and our commitment to the faith community to which we belong. These are the meanings of our contributing to the Church. In addition, what we give does return to us in one way or another.

Gospel Reading

The inside meaning of things is the theme of today's Gospel reading. Jesus criticizes religious practices performed only for public display. In the Catholic Church, we have a marvelous tradition of translating our faith into symbols, gestures and rituals: incense, vestments, color, devotions, Gregorian and contemporary church music. We must take great care that these traditions do not ossify into semi-automatic reflexes. It is vital that we nourish the living faith that gives substance to genuflections, signs of peace and ceremonies as well as to the money we place into the collection basket.

Point

We should not debase our religious traditions into ideological talismans. They live primarily as expressions of a living faith.

THURSDAY — Eleventh Week of the Year
2 Cor 11:1-11 *Mt 6:7-15*

First Reading

The change in mood in this section of Paul's letter is so stark that many have seen this as a distinct writing called the "severe letter" which had been sent to the Corinthians when Paul's problems with them were at a boil. In this reading, he contrasts himself with the slick preachers who were passing through Corinth. He tells the people to examine his life style. Unlike the others, he lives what he preaches. Secondly, he criticizes the Corinthians for their salad bar approach to the smorgasbord of teachings to which they had been exposed. At this early point in the Church's history, of course, there was no settled orthodoxy as we know it today. This fluidity, however, did not exonerate the Corinthians from a careful appraisal of what they had heard.

Today we are exposed to a variety of techniques in the area of religion. There is nothing inherently wrong with technique; the classic spiritual writers were its masters. Method, however, is auxiliary to the very demanding work of nurturing a spiritual life. A solid enduring spirituality requires dying to self. Exclusive reliance on technique can lead to a surface religiosity full of drama but devoid of insight.

Gospel Reading

There has been an explosion in the number of books published about prayer and prayer techniques today. In this Gospel reading, Jesus gives us a pattern of distinctively Christian prayer with an emphasis on quality over quantity. Matthew records a liturgical elaboration of Luke's version of the "Our Father." It really is an outline of the components of Christian prayer: we present our needs to God who is as close to us as a Father while submitting ourselves to His over-all design. Discerning God's will for us is the most difficult part of prayer. Technique can put us in a position to begin some spiritual rewiring. But to be able to say, "Thy will be done," can only emerge from the very core of a person after much spiritual labor.

Point

There is no short cut to spiritual vigor. It requires not only craft but conversion.

FRIDAY — Eleventh Week of the Year
2 Cor 11:18, 21-30   *Mt 6:19-23*

First Reading

Paul answers criticism of his work that had been made by various itinerant preachers. One charge was that he was not a Palestinian Jew as were the Apostles. Paul responds that he is as much an Israelite of Abraham's seed as are his critics. He adds that his sufferings as an Apostle are more telling than his family background. They are the ultimate credential. We can empathize with Paul's experience when we realize the lengths to which people go to retain their Catholic identity in South America and Africa — places of virulent persecution. To be identifiably Christian in many parts of the world can seriously jeopardize income and career. Yet, for these individuals, their faith is one thing that no regime can expropriate.

Although most of us are from Catholic families, more important than how our parents and grandparents responded to Christ is how we answer the call of the Lord which is specifically addressed to us.

Gospel Reading

The Lord asks whether God or property is the fulcrum of our lives. Although both play a vital role in our lives, one of them will be the lens through which we view the world. If property is at the center of our lives, then our religion becomes a subtle way of insuring the survival of what we have accumulated. If God is at our center, then the things we own enhance the ways we give glory to God. Whichever serves as our lens will color our view of the rest of the world.

Point

Everything we own today will someday belong to someone else. Our relationship with the Lord, which we have shaped over a lifetime, remains with us through life, death and into eternity.

SATURDAY — Eleventh Week of the Year
2 Cor 12:1-10   Mt 6:24-34

First Reading

Paul's defense of his ministry continues. Yesterday, he described the physical sufferings he endured as part of his credentials. Today, he points to a personal religious experience as another piece of evidence. It was an indescribable, mystical "out of the body" experience in which he felt transported to the third (or "seventh") heaven — very close to God. A physical ailment (eye trouble? epilepsy?) brought him crashing back to earth from these mystical heights. Oddly, this malady makes his point. It was precisely because Paul could not rely on the props of an attractive appearance, forensic eloquence or mystical experiences that the success of his preaching proved it to be God's power at work through him.

There are many holy people who are neither physically attractive nor great speakers. Those very disabilities allow the Holy Spirit to become all the more transparent through them.

Gospel Reading

Jesus speaks about the birds and flowers to make a point regarding the allocation of our spiritual resources. We should direct our energy into the personal and spiritual growth God intends for us and not into material substitutes. We can easily be distracted into collecting such substitutes: books in place of wisdom, 'contacts' in place of friends, trendy fashion in place of personal depth, boulevard gossip in place of social awareness. The same phenomenon can occur in the spiritual life. Efforts to collect religious artifacts and objects d'art can displace personal prayer and conversion.

Point

Counterfeit surrogates for spiritual life can only yield counterfeit experiences. Facsimiles have no power to save.

MONDAY — Twelfth Week of the Year
Gn 12:1-9   *Mt 7:1-5*

First Reading

Today, we begin the saga of Abraham. Against Genesis' epic backdrop of the fracture of the human race from God in the stories of Adam and Eve, Cain and Abel, the Flood and the Tower of Babel comes the call to Abraham to "leave this place." Now, the healing begins. "To leave this place" captures in a single phrase the themes of the Old and New Testaments — to abandon the old ways of sin, selfishness and the feud.

The geographical journey of the old man Abraham was a few hundred miles from Haran to Canaan. His spiritual journey, and that of Israel, was infinitely greater. He left behind his old deities and began a quest for the living God. The Old Testament documents this dawning sense of God and self. Abraham's spiritual journey continues today as we move from mutual exploitation and violence toward becoming a people of God.

Gospel Reading

We are all on a journey to that world described in today's Gospel reading — a world freed of prejudice where we are not quick to label and judge, where we respect each other as brothers and sisters. How we judge others reveals a great deal about ourselves and our view of God. The promised land is not a piece of real estate but a condition of soul. Like Abraham, we have been promised marvelous things if we leave our old ways. We have been promised intimacy with God, life without end and the capacity to channel God's life to others.

Point

We have all traveled a long way since our baptism. This is a journey available even to shut-ins. It is the journey of faith.

TUESDAY — Twelfth Week of the Year
Gn 13:2, 5-18   *Mt 7:6, 12-14*

First Reading

Abraham and Lot have prospered in Canaan and friction grows among their herdsmen. Abraham suggests a separation with first choice of location given to Lot. In a biblical version of "manifest destiny," Abraham and Lot seem to have taken over the land as they parcel it out between themselves with scant regard for the local natives. Ironically, Lot acts in his apparent self-interest to choose what seems the better land in which was situated a picturesque town called Sodom with its attractive suburb of Gomorrah. Abraham remains on the plain where God reiterates and expands the promise to him. Even Lot's selfish choice will not frustrate God's promise to Abraham. God threads His will through all the events of our life.

Gospel Reading

The Sermon on the Mount in Matthew's Gospel is actually a collection of various ad hoc teachings of Jesus: "Enter by the narrow gate"; "Treat others as you would have them treat you"; "Do not cast your pearls before swine." The purpose of this last admonition was not to validate religious elitism but to preserve the Gospel from trivialization. We are not faced today with the external Jewish opposition that ostracized Matthew's community. More ominous for us is the internal threat that comes from an easy commercialization and dilution of our tradition. Our rich, centuries-old Catholic tradition can easily be collapsed into the mold of a recent past that denigrates anything beyond itself.

Point

Abraham attempted to avoid suicidal fratricide in the middle of a hostile country. We should cherish and protect the integrity of our rich, full and dynamic Catholic tradition.

WEDNESDAY — Twelfth Week of the Year
Gn 15:1-12, 17-18   Mt 7:15-20

First Reading

This is the covenant. The Bible traces the roots of the Sinai covenant between God and the Israelite nation to this moment between God and Abraham. The meaning of this strange desert ritual of "cutting a covenant" seems to involve the invocation of a disaster, similar to what had befallen the slain animals, upon the party who breaks the deal. God alone passes through the carcasses because the agreement is unilateral. God is discovered here not to be capricious. He decided to bind Himself by the covenant and bestowed the promise on Abraham as a gift and not because of any reciprocity on Abraham's part.

As we reread these Genesis stories, we may wonder that Abraham's faith seems to tremble so often on the edge of doubt. When we know the outcome of events, nostalgia has great decorative power to romanticize the past. Abraham could not see the future. His only basis for faith was God's promise as symbolized by this primitive Eastern ritual.

Gospel Reading

The Lord gives us a quick course in distinguishing between true and fraudulent prophets. We need prophets to highlight God's presence to us. Yet, prophets of every stripe abound and to test them requires some skillful use of criteria. Like Abraham, we cannot "fast forward" in time to see who is right.

The first measure Jesus gives is to look at a person's life style — whether a prophet practices what he preaches. Does a person's pulpit word resonate in his or her life? The second test is to examine what a prophet offers: cheap grace, easy religion, shallow spiritual experiences — or the demanding avenue of personal conversion and soul-exposing prayer.

Point

We cannot judge the present with the same clarity with which we see the past. We must stand on the Lord's presence to us in the Church and sacraments.

THURSDAY — Twelfth Week of the Year
Gn 16:1-12, 15-16   Mt 7:21-29

First Reading

The Abraham epic moves forward as Abraham's preoccu-

pation with having a son causes Sarah to suggest his using
Hagar as a surrogate mother. Abraham quickly agrees. The son
is named Ishmael whom the Bible calls a "wild ass of a man" —
the father of the Arabs. The conflicts between Sarah and Hagar
and between Isaac and Ishmael speak on several levels. It is the
ancient Israelites' way of showing that the tensions between
Arabs and Jews have roots that go way back. At the same time, it
is an acknowledgment that through the common link with
Abraham, the Arabs still share in a special divine favor.

Abraham tries to arrange his own fulfillment of God's
promise to him. Despite our best efforts to manage details of
our life, God takes us on strange detours to His own fulfillment
of His promise to us.

Gospel Reading

Jesus' lesson in weeding out false prophets continues as
He concludes the Sermon on the Mount. He points out that a
prophet's spiritual pyrotechnics (exorcisms, miracles, charismatic experiences) do not by themselves guarantee the fullness
of spiritual life which comes exclusively from personal union
with Him. Holiness is not quantifiable into the number of
prayers, good works or spiritual phenomena we may produce.
Its hallmark is the solid base of internal transformation in how
we think and act, guided by the Lord's teaching.

Point

*Our special relationship with Jesus is indestructible be-
cause it lasts as long as we do.*

FRIDAY — Twelfth Week of the Year
Gn 17:1, 9-10, 15-22   *Mt 8:1-4*

First Reading

Abraham remains absorbed in the whereabouts of his

promised heir. Ishmael, the son born to the slave girl, is given a backdoor blessing with the assurance that he will not obstruct the promise and that the promise will not hinder his future. Facing the facts of his own and Sarah's advanced age, Abraham requests that the promised blessings be routed through Ishmael — the son he can see — rather than through a promised son still unborn.

Abraham is consistently held up to us as a man who believed against all probability that his God can give the gift of life to anyone at any age.

Gospel Reading

We see Jesus putting the Sermon on the Mount into practice. Leprosy, in any form, evoked the same horror in biblical times that it does today. We seem to have a visceral revulsion from lepers — as though their souls had been turned inside out and their sins exposed in the lesions of their skin. That, at least, is the superstition at the base of the fear and loathing heaped upon them in every culture that treated them as outcasts and as the living dead. It is a splendid detail in today's reading that Jesus stretched out His hand and *touched* the leper. In that single gesture, the Lord reached across pre-judices and misconceptions that spanned centuries. That touch is symbolic of Jesus' reaching out to release His saving power through the barriers we construct.

Point

Our God is a God of life and healing. No age, disease or social stigma, however ancient or modern, can force us outside the circle of His love.

SATURDAY — Twelfth Week of the Year
Gn 18:1-15   *Mt 8:5-17*

First Reading

The Word of God comes to each of us in many ways and for different reasons. In the first reading, Abraham shows hospitality to three passing strangers. One of the visitors in the story represents God and forecasts the birth of Abraham's long-anticipated son to Sarah in a year.

The Word of God comes to Abraham from a completely unexpected source to give him hope and assurance. That Word of God to him came true.

Gospel Reading

The Word of God in the Gospel reading comes as a word of healing for the centurion's servant, Peter's mother-in-law and the woman in the crowd. The Word of God is not confined to homilies or religious booklets. It comes to us in many disguises. However it may be clothed, we must first be receptive enough to recognize it. We can see such openness in Abraham's hospitality and in the centurion's faith.

God's Word comes to us not only for glorious and grand enterprises but also for the incidental pieces of daily living that few others may consider significant. Jesus not only taught doctrine and forgave sin. He also healed infirmities of every kind. God's Word assures, heals, inspires, comforts, reveals — it enhances every aspect of our life. Its scope is not narrowly religious.

Point

God's Word to us is not simply informational. It is found whenever and however the Spirit touches our life.

MONDAY — Thirteenth Week of the Year
Gn 18:16-33   *Mt 8:18-22*

First Reading

Sodom and Gomorrah were not even nice places to visit. A tragedy lurks beneath the humor of Abraham's haggling with God: not even ten good people could be found in Sodom and Gomorrah. What could these few, these ten, have accomplished? They might have served as reminders, much like a speed sign which can be disobeyed or disregarded. Such people set a standard. There are many good people among us who spend their lives in simple, direct and unheralded acts of kindness. They are lights that illuminate the darkness of our self-absorption. There were no lights in Sodom and Gomorrah.

Gospel Reading

This chapter of Matthew's Gospel is packed with miracles: the cleansed leper, the healed servant of the centurion, Peter's mother-in-law, the lake storm and exorcisms. In the middle of all this, a scribe comes forward to follow Jesus. Perhaps Matthew considers the scribe's interest to be itself a miracle. Jesus cautions him to be realistic about the implications of his request and not to be swept away by emotion. Our life and faith decisions should be intelligent and clear-sighted. The emotionally charged ambience of religious seasons and ceremonies can lead to sudden enthusiasms which distract from the hard thinking we must pursue about the consequences of serious discipleship.

Point

Being a light to others is a way of serving the Lord.

TUESDAY — Thirteenth Week of the Year
Gn 19:15-29   Mt 8:23-27

First Reading

Lot's wife truly was the salt of the earth. The point of this bizarre incident is surely not that anyone who sins will be turned into salt. Originally, this was a floating piece of legend built around the natural salt stalagmites near the Dead Sea. Perhaps one formation resembled a human being. Many rock formations in the Western part of the United States have sufficient human similarities that they give rise to strange stories of their origins. The memory of some tragedy that befell Lot's wife attached to a particular salt formation. The Bible uses this legend to make the theological point that there is judgment not only on defiance of God but on indecision as well. The hesitation of Lot's wife is contrasted with Abraham's faith.

Gospel Reading

The Gospel reading reminds us of an important and perhaps counterintuitive truth. The Lord Jesus is present in the various storms of our life. We instinctively see the problems we face as indications of God's absence or disfavor. The insight which Matthew offers is a powerful comfort: the Lord is with us in the very middle of the storm. In the complexity of our lives, we seldom have the data we would like to make a decision. The best we can do is consult, pray, decide and then go forward. Having done our best, we can be assured that Jesus remains with us in whatever follows.

Point

The Lord gives us strength to survive the storms of our life.

WEDNESDAY — Thirteenth Week of the Year
Gn 21:5, 8-20   Mt 8:28-34

First Reading

In today's first reading, Hagar, the Egyptian slave girl, is summarily dismissed in common Oriental fashion. In reading the Old Testament, we should recall that the patriarchs are not held up for us as ideal role models of human compassion. Their significance lies not in what they shared with the surrounding cultures but in the ways they differed. There is an incremental step forward here in Abraham's concern for Hagar, a refreshing parenthesis in the brutal story of that age.

Hagar receives a word from God that her son, about seventeen years old by now, will have a greatness of his own. In some incalculable way, salvation history will touch those outside the genetic line from Abraham through Isaac to Jacob. Indeed, Abraham was to be a blessing for all peoples. That promise came true in Christ.

Gospel Reading

Most probably, Jesus is in non-Jewish territory since there would be no reason for kosher Jews to keep swine. The exorcism He performs is not recounted to prove the existence of diabolic possession but to accentuate Jesus' power in His ministry as well as in the Church today. After this demonstration of His power, however, the townspeople asked Him to depart either because they were afraid of Him or saw Him as a threat to the local economy. This is one of the very few instances where a miracle among the Gentiles failed to elicit faith.

Point

Faith is not an assured response to the presence of God.

The encounter with God mellowed Abraham but frightened the townspeople.

THURSDAY — Thirteenth Week of the Year
Gn 22:1-19   Mt 9:1-8

First Reading

This is a seismic event in the history of religion. This incident has a much deeper meaning than Abraham's passing a test of faith. Somewhere in the middle of Abraham's transition from his ancestral paganism to belief in the living God, a revelation comes to him that he is not to sacrifice his son. From this moment, human sacrifice would never more have a legitimate place in Israel's dealings with God. This is a quantum leap forward in man's understanding of God and of faith.

On a mountain called Moriah, somewhere in a desert of Judah, God made it clear to mankind that an obedient and faithful life is worth more than a thousand blood sacrifices.

Gospel Reading

Jesus forgives a person's sin. The Jewish teachers believed there was a direct correlation between the amount of sin in a person's soul and the amount of illness in a person's body. Jesus proves that the man's sins are forgiven in the only way the Jewish teachers could comprehend. He heals the man.

Of course, the healthiest people are not necessarily the holiest. Still, spiritual disharmony can affect a person's general well-being. Peace at our center shows itself through our emotions, minds, bodies and dealings with others. Conversely, disharmony within us also evidences itself in every sector of our lives. The recounting of this incident was vital for the early Church because absolution from sin was not part of the Jewish heritage. It was the Easter gift of Jesus to the community He founded.

Point

Ancient sacrifices were offered in the belief that the healing of the rift between the community and God would have a positive effect on the individual. Jesus heals the rift between the individual and God and this has a ripple effect on society.

FRIDAY — Thirteenth Week of the Year
Gn 23:1-4, 19; 24:1-8, 62-67   *Mt 9:9-13*

First Reading

Although the story of Abraham comes to an end, the story of the promise goes on. The Bible tells us that Abraham was 138 years old when he buried Sarah and later married a woman named Keturah. Clearly, he was not only a man of great faith but of high hopes as well. There must have been lots of Vitamin E in the hill country of Judea.

In today's reading, Abraham arranges the marriage of Isaac. He insists that Isaac marry among his own people and not with the Canaanites. A servant is sent spouse-hunting and discovers Rebecca. He puts a ring in her nose and pays off her family. The reading ends with the comment that Isaac loved Rebecca. Later episodes would seem to indicate that she had more affection for her younger son Jacob than she had for either Isaac or Esau. In all these seemingly disconnected and very human events, the promise continues to take shape together with a people.

Gospel Reading

Jesus seems to do the very opposite of Abraham. While

Abraham stresses isolation from non-Jews, Jesus goes to the outcasts — tax collectors and prostitutes. Each incident in the Bible is part of a larger movement. The Old Testament portrays the coalescence of a people to keep the covenant and to carry forward the promise. Matthew describes Jesus' retrieval of the ancient Jewish covenant tradition in a new synthesis centered in His own teaching and ministry. Jesus is the new Israel who now reaches out to all people to join them into a family linked not by genes but by faith in Him. The Lord's reference to the prophet Hosea puts into words the profound difference between Christ and the Pharisees and between Christianity and Pharisaism. We do not become righteous in order to approach God; we approach God to become righteous.

Point

The difference between seeing events in our lives as atomized or connected is the Spirit. The Holy Spirit helps us see the connections.

SATURDAY — Thirteenth Week of the Year
Gn 27:1-5, 15-29   *Mt 9:14-17*

First Reading

Jacob gets his father's blessing by fraud. Perhaps Isaac wanted to be tricked. In the tension between Jacob and Esau, the Bible sees a model of the conflict between farmers and hunters as well as between Israelites and Edomites. The blessing of God is perceived here as a kind of spiritual prize transmitted from one person to another which could be stolen, hoarded or bartered away. Jacob finally grabbed the blessing and ran. The result: Rebecca alienated her older son Esau and would never see her favorite son Jacob again; Jacob became a fugitive; Isaac is deceived in his old age; Esau seeks revenge. In the middle of all this family treachery, the story of the promise continues.

Gospel Reading

Many of the sayings collected in Matthew's Gospel glow with the half-life of now-forgotten debates that rocked the early Church, especially concerning its relations with Judaism. Here, Jesus speaks about new wine and new wineskins. The Gospel is not an overhauled version of Judaism. It brings about a qualitatively new relationship between God and people. The Old Testament is preserved in the Church not from antiquarian interest but because it helps to illuminate the meaning of the Lord Jesus. The community Jesus founded is now the heir of all the Old Testament promises. Hence, Matthew's emphasis on keeping old and new. The Old Testament stories, even the most brutal ones, provide the very human background of a people from whom came Jesus of Nazareth. The Old Testament contains the Lord's cultural and theological background. Further, in the light of Jesus, the Holy Spirit speaks to us through the Old Testament experience.

Point

The Holy Spirit cannot be sold or exchanged. The Spirit of God, so prized by Jacob, is now available for free to all believers through the power of the Resurrection. This is the heart of the new covenant.

MONDAY — Fourteenth Week of the Year
Gn 28:10-22   Mt 9:18-26

First Reading

This incident provides the theme for the spiritual, "We are Climbing Jacob's Ladder" as well as the verses of "Nearer, My

God, to Thee." Jacob is on the run after stealing Esau's birthright blessing. Even in the middle of our interpersonal treacheries, God will reveal Himself. This place would eventually become the famous northern Israelite shrine of Bethel, a place where God and people meet (the stairway). Jacob sets up a stone as a memorial of this overwhelming experience of God. The human impulse to create shrines and to remember special moments expresses itself in lovers' initials carved on a tree as well as in a soaring basilica. It is not the place but the experience it memorializes that is sacred. We call the place holy because it recalls and perhaps revives the original experience.

Gospel Reading

In today's Gospel reading, the Lord heals in the street as well as in the synagogue leader's house. All places are made holy by the presence of Jesus. We all have locations we cherish because they recall public events or personal turning points in our lives. The memories they evoke can breathe new vitality into a tired faith. They cannot replace, however, the living and believing we must do in the present. They recall the past to energize the present.

Point

Experiences make places holy.

TUESDAY — Fourteenth Week of the Year
Gn 32:23-33   Mt 9:32-38

First Reading

This curious incident is a blend of folklore and Jewish theology. Precisely what occurred at the riverside is unclear. But it changed Jacob. Before this surreal experience, Jacob was a wheeling-dealing rogue. By masquerading as Esau, he stole a birthright from his blind father; by a primitive form of genetic engineering, he had double-crossed his treacherous father-in-law, Laban. Now, he is told that Esau is coming to see him with a squad of 400 men — an opportune moment for a religious experience.

There was a semi-physical/spiritual struggle that transformed Jacob. He is now named Israel and begins to behave like a patriarch of a great nation. A clear spiritual sight emerged out of that struggle.

Gospel Reading

The Gospel reading reminds us that the wrestling with faith through which we all have gone can be a way of shepherding others. We all struggle to find God in our life. Such searchings are so common that an entire descriptive vocabulary has arisen within our tradition to describe them: "dark night of the soul," "spiritual aridity," "loss of consolation." If we pursue such times to their conclusion, we can emerge from them with a deeper and clearer sight.

Point

What we learn through our struggles with darkness can help others to see light. It can be our way of bringing in the harvest.

WEDNESDAY — Fourteenth Week of the Year
Gn 41:55-57; 42:5-7, 17-24   *Mt 10:1-7*

First Reading

The first reading enters the middle of the Joseph story. Joseph was the youngest and most favored of Jacob's twelve sons. He had a penchant for singularly self-centered dreams that offended his brothers and delighted his father. His jealous brothers sold him into slavery where his knack for interpreting dreams raised him to the position of economic advisor to Egypt's Pharaoh.

A famine forced Jacob's family to immigrate to Egypt where they would grow into a great people. The later conflicts among the tribes of Israel are captured in the conflicts among the brothers. Slowly, the promise to Abraham is coming true.

Gospel Reading

Because the Jewish Christians were dismayed over the influx of Gentiles into the Church, Matthew records the words of the Lord instructing the Apostles to go first to all the people of Israel. Jesus' earthly ministry, which Matthew depicts as limited to Israel, will be catapulted into the Gentile world after the Resurrection. The Lord sent this first mission to the Jewish people because His death and Resurrection would fulfill the ancient promises made to them. The meaning of Easter is best seen by recalling Old Testament history, as we do at the Easter Vigil. The Old Testament is the key to the meaning of Jesus. All that was religiously significant in the old covenant passed over into the Lord Jesus.

Point

Our religious and personal past conditions our thinking about faith and God. Our past can tell us a great deal about God's plan for our individual futures.

THURSDAY — Fourteenth Week of the Year
Gn 44:18-21, 23-29; 45:1-5   Mt 10:7-15

First Reading

The Joseph story ends happily as Joseph forgives his brothers. Christians have long seen a model or preview of

Christ in Joseph. He is betrayed by his own and forgives them. The story reminds us that forgiveness liberates both the one who forgives as well as the one forgiven. So often, we replay the tapes of past hurts and await an opportunity to even the score. Forgiving others is not effortless. We come to terms emotionally with our decision to forgive only after a protracted period of time. Gradually, it will free us from the domination of the past and the cancer of hatred that can infect our every waking moment.

Gospel Reading

Jesus gives a missionary instruction to the Apostles. Its theme is one of not getting tied down to real estate or personal possessions. He tells His disciples to remove anything that can weigh them down physically or psychologically. Even the indifference and rejection of people must be put aside. They must keep their eyes on the Gospel message and not divert their energies into anything ancillary. People's salvation is to be the central consideration.

Point

We must not let past wrongs control, trap and blind us to the need to forgive. Forgiving others sets us free.

FRIDAY — Fourteenth Week of the Year
Gn 46:1-7, 28-30   Mt 10:16-23

First Reading

Jacob and his family finally leave the land promised them for Egypt where they will become a great nation. Jacob and Joseph will die there (and be the only people in the Old Testament to be embalmed). Jacob's dying words to his sons describe the historical fortunes of the various tribes during the time of the Judges. "Reuben (an unreliable tribe), you are wild as the waves of the sea; you will be first no longer. . . Simon (a tribe that disappeared) and Levi (a social class without land), you are men of violence and injustice . . . your descendants will be scattered. . . Judah (the tribe of David and Jesus), you sit like a lion . . . the scepter will not depart from you until he comes whom everyone will obey." In a slow shift to the Exodus story, we see the diversity of the tribes. The attainment of nationhood would not be easy. Uniting these people required strength, charisma and discipline.

Gospel Reading

We have here an echo of the experience of the early Christians in the generations after Christ when it was dangerous to be Christian. They were hunted by the state, rejected by the religious establishment and ridiculed by their families. The Lord tells His followers to avoid pointless martyrdom. In such adversity, it took a great deal of leadership to keep these early Christian communities united. Today we are faced with challenges to discipleship from religious pluralism, affluence and secular hegemony. It also takes intelligent and Spirit-filled leadership to keep us united in what is essential.

Point

As it took a great deal of effort to keep Israel and the early Church united, so it takes discipline to keep the different parts of our life together. We have to struggle to keep ourselves at spiritual peace.

SATURDAY — Fourteenth Week of the Year
Gn 49:29-33; 50:15-24   Mt 10:24-33

First Reading

The patriarch Jacob dies. The brothers of Joseph immediately suspect that Joseph will now reveal his true feelings which they assume he has until now shrewdly concealed. This is not the case as Joseph's forgiveness was genuine and not a ruse. What this reading illustrates is the difficulty many of us have in believing that we are really forgiven, that God carries no grudge, that our sins are forgiven forever — they do not come back like invisible ink. Perhaps the brothers were projecting their own hardheartedness onto Joseph. But the reconciliation was genuine and family unity was restored. It was important that they accept forgiveness.

Gospel Reading

The Lord tells His disciples that their message and experience of God must be widely published. The Christian knowledge of God was not to be a secret or private experience. The number of people reached by Jesus physically in His lifetime was relatively small. His message would be kept alive and His ministry of healing continued through His followers. The Church is more than a witness to events that transpired twenty centuries ago. It is the Galilean ministry of Jesus brought to life every day all over the world.

Point

The world needs to hear of the power of forgiveness. Reconciliation among Christians is living proof of the Resurrection.

MONDAY — Fifteenth Week of the Year
Ex 1:8-14, 22   *Mt 10:34-11:1*

First Reading

A few critical events of our past — the Great Depression, the Second Vatican Council or a warmly remembered relationship — mold much of our outlook on life. Today, we begin the Book of Exodus, the very heart of the Old Testament. The events it describes — oppression in Egypt (today's first reading), release from bondage, wandering in the wilderness — form a privileged moment. Here the Israelites came to know the God of their fathers and themselves in a way that so seared itself into their souls that these events became the special angle from which they would view all later events.

Gospel Reading

If the Jewish experience of God revolved around the Exodus, then the life, death and Resurrection of Jesus is at the hub of the Christian universe. The words and deeds of Jesus as experienced, remembered and faithfully recorded in the Gospels provide the spiritual coordinates for us. In today's Gospel reading, we see that the early Church embraced faith in Christ with such passion that it led to a severe wrenching from their past and to deep intrafamily conflicts as well. When we tend to domesticate faith and to blunt its sharp edges, this reading reminds us of the seriousness with which we must take our relationship with the Lord if His Spirit is to transform us as He did the first Christians.

Point

Personal knowledge of Jesus is not a luxury. It is the heart of spiritual life. Its intensity defines who we are, where we stand with God and how far we have yet to travel to our promised land.

TUESDAY — Fifteenth Week of the Year
Ex 2:1-15   *Mt 11:20-24*

First Reading

The Israelites' bondage in Egypt is a powerful symbol. It

encompassed not only physical slavery but social dislocation, loss of purpose and a vanished sense of any special relationship with God. When Moses led Israel out of Egypt, he did much more than restore political freedom. He gave the Israelites a sense of community, an appreciation of their mission among the nations and, through the Sinai experience, a covenant with God. Freedom for Israel was more than physical. It had profound spiritual and moral implications.

A person can be politically free while remaining a slave to sin, drugs or powerful emotions. These are deeper and tighter chains which grip not only the body but the very soul of a person. It is no surprise that some people willingly exchange their political and economic liberty for some guru's promise of a synthetic inner liberation of the spirit.

Gospel Reading

Jesus speaks of judgment against three towns. We are not told what signs He displayed in their streets. We do know they brought judgment upon themselves by their refusal of His word.

Freedom is not a choice of whether we will worship but of which altar we will serve. Some people worship career, power, money or sexual attraction. These gods have such hypnotic power that their devotees will sacrifice anything, even the lives of those closest to them, to these gods of the marketplace. By contrast, we can serve the God of the Exodus and Easter who sets us free to enjoy the world and everything in it. This is a God who wants not slaves but sons and daughters.

Point

The three towns chose their judgment as we do when we choose our god. Every person becomes like the god he or she serves.

WEDNESDAY — Fifteenth Week of the Year
Ex 3:1-6, 9-12   *Mt 11:25-27*

First Reading

Moses had married Zipporah and had a son named Gershom. As the first reading tells us, Jethro was his father-in-law. Cecil B. De Mille's movie, *The Ten Commandments,* made a great deal more out of this virtually unknown segment of Moses' life than does the Bible.

In this reading, Moses discovers God. Until this point, he was not an irreligious man. Like many of his own and our contemporaries, however, it seems that he had never seriously adverted to God's pervasive presence — until now. This is the moment when God discloses Himself to Moses in a dramatic way. Moses becomes "involved" with God for the first time.

Gospel Reading

Against the background of three towns indifferent to His word, Jesus thanks the Father, almost in Johannine fashion, for revealing to His humble and unlearned followers what the sophisticated would not see.

A person who treats God as nothing more than a notion to be analyzed cannot experience the power of God's presence. He has reduced God to another item in his conceptual inventory upon which to muse at leisure. For such an individual, the bush does not burn. On the other hand, a person who becomes "involved" with God and strives to claim the promise (as did Abraham and Jacob) is changed through the struggle. He or she has begun to enter the only relationship that has power to give eternal life.

Point

Faith does not require the surrender of our rationality. It requires self-surrender.

THURSDAY — Fifteenth Week of the Year
Ex 3:11-20   *Mt 11:28-30*

First Reading

This is one of the most cryptic passages of the Bible. Moses asks the name of God. We still do not know the precise meaning of the reply. It has been variously translated. "I am . . . who am . . . that I am . . . that cause to be . . . who will be with you." This was the word too sacred to use for which Jews substituted *Adonai*. Centuries later, that mysterious word, known today as *Yahweh*, was mispronounced as *Jehovah*, afterward translated into Greek as *Kyrios* and then into Latin as *Dominus*. This name, which Moses never in fact uses, is revealed to signify Moses' knowledge of God born from this encounter.

This reading is saturated with the deep mystery of God. Moses and the people will come to know this God through the events of their deliverance as well as through their later history. We come to know this God from the slice of the universe which we inhabit, from the story and teachings of Jesus and through our own personal history. Yet, whenever we think we have corralled God into sacred groves and objects, we are usually humbled by the elusive mystery of the great "I am."

Gospel Reading

The Lord speaks to those struggling to find God and desperately trying to live according to His will. To people who were going crazy from the complex architecture of regulations imposed on them ostensively to help them organize their spiritual lives, Jesus says, "If you're exhausted from all this, come to me. I will refresh you. My way is easy. Follow me. Just do what I do. Live in me." The same sacred intimacy with God that was granted to Moses at the bush through the holy name is now available to us through Jesus.

Point

The theological analysis of God is complex. The experience is simple. Trust the experience.

FRIDAY — Fifteenth Week of the Year
Ex 11:10-12:14   *Mt 12:1-8*

First Reading

God's instruction for the Passover celebration prescribes its annual observance. As we read these words, we are witnessing the transformation of Israel's Exodus moment into a liturgical event. As a result, future generations who were not present in these epochal days will be able to share the experience through ritual. The devout Jew believes that in some mysterious way through the power of this rite of Passover, he or she becomes a participant in that original Exodus. Of course, as years go on, this Passover celebration will accumulate many meanings. There will be new Pharaohs and different Egypts. When the Lord celebrated the Passover at the Last Supper, He celebrated a new and final liberation of mankind from the Egypt of sin and death. The promise to Moses was complete.

Gospel Reading

The differences between Jesus and the Jewish leaders continue to grow. The Mishnah, a collection of rabbinic opinions, states that "the rules about Sabbath . . . are as mountains hanging by a hair, for Scripture is scanty and the rules many" (Hag 1.8). The issue of picking grain surfaces a deeper conflict. Different views of God, of religion and of the place of human beings in the universe are in collision here. Is man to be a slave of the Sabbath or is the Sabbath for man? Are human beings to be servants of a system, religious or otherwise, or is the purpose of religion to emancipate us for an intimate, free and energizing relationship with God?

Point

In our Christian Passover, we celebrate our freedom in Christ to speak anywhere, anytime to the God of the galaxies and to call Him . . . Father!

SATURDAY — Fifteenth Week of the Year
Ex 12:37-42   Mt 12:14-21

First Reading

At last, we have *the* Exodus, the release. We all remember the scene from *The Ten Commandments* in which the Israelites assembled by tribe awaiting the signal to move forward from Charlton Heston. Scholars question whether it was all so orderly. But the details are not important. The Exodus is a cinemascopic/technicolor model of what God does in every person's life. That is why we have the enduring celebration of the Passover.

As they left Egypt, many may have dreamed of tribal prestige, wealth and easy entry into the promised land. None of these were to be the abiding outcome of the Exodus. Its purpose was spiritual — the covenant. By keeping faith in their God alive through the centuries, the Israelites would be the vanguard of the spiritual transformation of the human race.

Gospel Reading

Jesus and the Pharisees are in conflict; Jesus withdraws; He heals; He instructs His followers in the politically volatile atmosphere of Messianic expectancy not to breathe a word of this. . . . Matthew looked back at these happenings and applies to Jesus what he remembered Isaiah had said about a mysterious servant of God: "The bruised reed he will not crush, the smoldering wick he will not quench." Matthew expresses a great insight of the early Church. The Messiah did not come in coercive power but as Isaiah's sympathetic, helping servant of God. His ministry was not to be political but spiritual.

Point

God gives hope to the discouraged and strength to the weary — the bruised reeds and smoldering wicks among us. The real power of the God of the Exodus is found not only in that single event but in His continuing presence among His people as their source of life, strength and light.

MONDAY — Sixteenth Week of the Year
Ex 14:5-18   *Mt 12:38-42*

First Reading

In today's first reading, the magnificent deliverance seems to be coming unglued as Pharaoh's posse approaches the Israelites. The people turn on Moses in the first of their many complaints that slavery was preferable to and safer than this journey of faith. God instructs Moses to move the Israelites forward as the menace of Pharaoh's army is turned into proof of God's saving presence. The vice of the Israelites accented by Exodus is their constant demand for exciting new evidence of God's love at every stage of the way instead of trusting in the promise. Whenever such evidence is not immediately forthcoming, the grumbling, mumbling and hankering for Egypt resumed.

Gospel Reading

The demand for a sign continues in today's Gospel reading. Jesus answers that the only sign the leaders will receive is one like that of Jonah's preaching or Solomon's wisdom. The words of Jesus are self-authenticating to those who live in the spirit and not simply the letter of the Old Testament. For those who seek a sign, Jesus' life, death and Resurrection comprise the ultimate key to His identity. Many people see God as removed from the regular operation of the universe. They see Him only in the abnormal. They see no sign of God in the majesty of the stars, the intricacy of the human body, the reach of the human mind or the complex elegance of the natural world. Instead, they choose to see evidence of God only in icons that blink and statues that bleed.

Point

If we look to the pattern of events in our lives rather than isolated happenings, we will discover that God is near.

TUESDAY — Sixteenth Week of the Year
Ex 14:21-15:1   *Mt 12:46-50*

First Reading

This is the most dramatic part of the Exodus: the passage through the Red Sea. "The wind blew throughout the night . . . the water was like a wall." Did it happen like the movie? All the Israelites knew was that they were on the brink of extermination; wind parted the waters; they went through safely; the Egyptians did not. Was it natural or supernatural? Such a distinction was not domestic to the Hebrew mind. Natural events can flow together in such a way that they show forth in a vivid way God's enduring love for us. That is the essence of a miracle. It is less a suspension of the natural laws of physics and chemistry than it is a confluence of natural events in such a way as to illustrate the providential care of God that is always there.

The destruction of the Egyptian army marks a new stage in the life of Israel. From this point, they are no longer escaping refugees. They are now confronted with the burden of freedom. Nevertheless, this was a great moment when a narrow escape united them in an experience that would be remembered, recited and celebrated.

Gospel Reading

Perhaps the truly significant bonds that join people are not biological but spiritual: the shared experiences of school, seminary, war, political campaigns, joy, sorrow or deliverance. Jesus tells us that those who listen to and keep His word are His brothers and, He adds, "sisters" in a new family knit together by the Holy Spirit. We have all experienced deliverance through baptism. That, more than geography or nationality, is the true basis of Christian community.

Point

Passage through the Red Sea marked a new stage in Israel's becoming a people of God. Our baptism is also the beginning of a process of our maturing in the Lord.

WEDNESDAY — Sixteenth Week of the Year
Ex 16:1-5, 9-15   *Mt 13:1-9*

First Reading

After the deliverance from Egyptian oppression, the desert wandering began. Here in the desert of Sin (Zin), the Israelites cursed their liberation as they longed for the delicacies of

Egypt. It was better to be a slave in the city than to be free in the desert.

The manna and quail are periodic desert phenomena. Moses enabled the people to see this as a sign of God's presence rather than a freak of nature or a bit of good luck. Later, in the eleventh chapter of the Book of Numbers, they will quickly tire of this manna. It is important to remember that the Israelites had no distinctive, coherent religion back in Egypt. There were no rabbis, no synagogues, no sacred books — only the haunting memory of a promise made to an ancestor. From this semi-heathen group, a deep and thriving spirituality would gradually emerge and be preserved in a remnant of people attuned to God. We know the names of some people who typified this remnant: Simeon, Anna, Joseph, Mary, Zechariah, Elizabeth, Joachim and Anne.

Gospel Reading

The parable of the seed was important to the early Church. The seed was broadcast all over. From the few seeds that fell on good ground sprang a fabulous harvest. Some of those seeds produced a stalk of 100 grains — a bonanza. This is perhaps the original point of the parable. Despite the wide range of human responses to God's Word, the Gospel thrives nevertheless.

Point

The Gospel parable reminds us that a deeply faithful minority can be the spiritual energy cell that drives an entire parish.

THURSDAY — Sixteenth Week of the Year
Ex 19:1-2, 9-11, 16-20   *Mt 13:10-17*

First Reading

In the first reading, the people prepare for the revelation of

God's glory. It is an awesome religious moment. This motley group of half-pagan people will emerge from this experience as a people of the covenant. Until now, they have known deliverance from oppression as a free gift of God. Here, at the mountain, they will begin to understand that such freedom has implications and makes demands as well.

Gospel Reading

In His teaching, Jesus begins to use parables, a standard device of wisdom teachers and rabbis. Parables had enormous suggestive power to trigger insight into the contours of the spiritual domain. The Lord may have spoken parables that have not been preserved. The ones recorded in the Gospels were deeply significant to the early Church and remain relevant to us.

Parables reveal the mysteries of the kingdom. "Mystery" means less a puzzle to be solved than a hidden dimension beneath the ordinary. In the early Church, baptism was preceded by a long period of preparation and a progressive initiation into the mysteries of faith. Today, the reverse is true. We are initiated into the mysteries of faith when we are young and spend the rest of our lives striving for understanding. Like the Israelites, we have experienced deliverance and now try to assimilate its implications.

Point

Parables help us to understand our Christian identity. Through them, the Holy Spirit reveals to us the mysteries of the kingdom — the presence of God within the ordinary and routine.

FRIDAY — Sixteenth Week of the Year
Ex 20:10-17   *Mt 13:18-23*

First Reading

The first reading recites the Ten Commandments. They state the sustaining conditions of deliverance, what the Israelites must do to keep themselves free and united as a people of God. These commandments will receive more expansive elaboration as the Israelites settle down to develop increasingly complex economic and social arrangements. Here in the desert, however, the prohibitions are simple and direct.

The sixth commandment, for example, has been the source of an elaborate sexual moral theology over the centuries. Originally, however, it probably prohibited a simple property crime. A man's wife was his property. To steal a wife was to steal property. Eventually, of course, this primitive desert rule received wider and more balanced interpretations.

Gospel Reading

The interpretation of the parable of the Sower's seed in today's Gospel reading illustrates an elaboration of the Lord's teaching by the early Church and the start of a long chain of such applications. Its original thrust was the abundant harvest despite the many failed seeds. The Church elaborated this story into a taxonomy of religious responses to the preached Gospel: the half-hearted, the superficial enthusiast, the frenetic and the sincere. The resonance of those categories in our own time is an assurance of the abiding constancy of human nature as well as the enduring challenge of preaching the Gospel.

Point

Faith and religion are not static. To keep the faith, we must let it grow.

SATURDAY — Sixteenth Week of the Year
Ex 24:3-8   Mt 13:24-30

First Reading

The people ratify the covenant with God. The deal is cut not with a single person, Abraham, but with the people. The blood of the sacrificed animals is splashed on the altar and upon the people. This mixing of blood is an old gesture signifying the union of two families.

The people will not change overnight. It was difficult for them to shed the ways of slaves and of the desert. In this covenant ceremony they started on a road. Despite failures and mistakes to come, the covenant will be a vehicle for moral regrouping. If at any one point we took a snapshot of Israel's soul, we would find ample covenant violations. If we examined the general direction in which they were moving as a people, we might see a different picture.

Gospel Reading

The Gospel parable of the wheat and weeds has several layers of meaning. We can take the viewpoint of the farmer. Because the roots of this type of wheat and weed intertwine, it is dangerous to pull out the weeds. The farmer decides to continue the crop despite the mixed results thus far. He was not so dismayed by the weeds as to destroy the entire harvest. If we take a moral snapshot of our lives, we will see virtue and vice intertwined. It is more important to look at the overall direction in which our life is going. Otherwise, a person can so focus on single instances of sin that they seem to overwhelm and hide the presence of grace in our lives.

Point

The general direction of our life rather than isolated acts is the most accurate measure of where we stand with the Lord.

MONDAY — Seventeenth Week of the Year
Ex 32:15-24, 30-34   *Mt 13:31-35*

First Reading

This was a thrilling scene in the movie, *The Ten Commandments,* and is really a model of Israel's historical struggle. The covenant is broken both by the people's adulation of the golden calf as well as by Moses' smashing of the tablets against the base of the mountain. Commandments etched in stone mean nothing when the people's hearts are turned away from the Lord they promised to serve. The plea of Moses on behalf of the people commences a long series of intercessors who will interpose themselves between the sins of the people and the justice of God. This prayer of intercession will wind its way through judges, kings and prophets until it finds its conclusion and fulfillment on a mound outside Jerusalem. By the prayer and death of Jesus a new covenant will be born and, with it, an enduring promise of forgiveness whenever and wherever people sincerely repent.

Gospel Reading

These two familiar images provide a stunning contrast with the Exodus reading. Jesus describes the growth of the kingdom from small beginnings. The tiny mustard seed grows into a gigantic tree into which people of every culture and from every nation can come home. Where the old covenant is pictured as born in majesty, thunder and lightning, the new covenant begins in ignominy and disgrace on Calvary. Despite their different births, the old covenant pretty much remains within the confines of Judaism while the new covenant continues to expand its reach. The second image of yeast is less obvious to us. Leaven was considered a corruption of unleavened bread. The Lord may be referring to the lower classes with which the early Church began, and to how the Spirit of Christ would transform such rude beginnings into a force that would change society. The kingdom will not grow by magic but by the Holy Spirit working through us.

Point

When Jesus' side was lanced on Calvary, His inmost Self flowed out into the Church. That divine love and not human faithfulness is the power of the new covenant.

TUESDAY — Seventeenth Week of the Year
Ex 33:7-11; 34:5-9, 28   Mt 13:35-43

First Reading

In the first reading, the place to meet the Lord God moves from the mountain to a transitional tent. In his conversation with God, Moses asks the Lord to accompany His people to the promised land and to allow him to see the divine glory face to face. Moses would not see the Lord face to face in his lifetime, but he would experience the glory. The tent would be the sign for all the people that God remained in their midst. One day, they would leave the holy mountain, but the Lord would be with them not in the fire and cloud but in the person of Moses and Joshua, and in the tent. We see in this scene a gradual relocation of the sign of God's presence from miraculous spectacle into enduring charismatic and liturgical symbols. The successors of Moses and the later versions of this primitive tent would be the tangible signs of the invisible presence of God.

Gospel Reading

This is a turning point in Matthew's Gospel. Jesus leaves

the crowds for a while and privately explains the parable of the good and bad crops to the disciples. The Lord's explanation is imbued with the vocabulary and imagery of the Old Testament. Both the followers of Christ and of the evil one will exist in the same world until the final separation at the end of the age. Until that time, much like the Israelites, we live in a time of liturgy and symbol. The full glory of the holy and the full horror of evil are seldom faced in their clearest light. Good is often caricatured as weakness while evil masquerades as success and fashion. Such inversions will continue to be part of the scene. Meanwhile, we live with parables and symbols awaiting the full display of God's power and glory.

Point

Because good and evil mingle in our world, we need vivid symbols and signs to serve as focal points for our faith and our life.

WEDNESDAY — Seventeenth Week of the Year
Ex 34:29-35   *Mt 13:44-46*

First Reading

This first reading is a famous scene in which Moses experiences the glory of God. Every Old Testament writer knew that to see God was beyond our human capacity. It was an experience unlike any other. Popular symbols to convey the mystery of God were storm, light, thunder and fire. When Moses emerges from God's presence, he is transfigured in an unearthly light as the glory of God was reflected in him. This incident provides part of the Old Testament background for the Lord's Transfiguration. An erroneous translation once said that Moses was "horned" rather than transformed. Some old pictures actually depicted him with horns. (That must have made for some extremely interesting sermons.) Moses was so changed that he veiled his face. When people experience the boundaries of ordinary life and look over its edge at deaths or births, for example, or whenever people meet the Lord — it changes them.

Gospel Reading

The Gospel reading tells us that our meeting the Lord Jesus is like finding a treasure or discovering a pearl. For some people, the reality of Christ hits them suddenly and decisively. For others, it is the result of a search. In both cases, an experience of the Lord changes them and compels them to reorganize their lives. We can note a difference between the two readings. Moses veiled his face to hide the glory. He was unapproachable. Since God became man in Jesus, the glory of God can shine through our humanity and look out through human features. The glory of God is seen not in awesome brilliance but in the Christlike humanity and approachability of people.

Point

The glory of God does not negate or swamp our humanity. It makes us into unique images of the Lord Jesus.

THURSDAY — Seventeenth Week of the Year
Ex 40:16-21, 34-38   *Mt 13:47-53*

First Reading

We come to the end of Exodus and the end of an era. Moses builds the Dwelling Place in which he places the ark as the glory of God descends upon it. God's presence has become institutionalized. He is no longer only the God of the burning bush or of the mountain. Now He dwells with His people as promised. While other religions have had their holy places, the ark travels with the people as they move to enter the promised land. The God of Israel is not a God of the place but of the people. Israel would always be a mixed bag but God's presence would not depart from them. He might be among them as a word of deliverance or a word of judgment but the Lord would not abandon His people.

Gospel Reading

God's presence among His people moved from Sinai to the tabernacle tent and now, through Jesus, as the pervasive Holy Spirit present in the community as well as in individual hearts. The dragnet pulls in every sort of fish to be later separated on shore. Like Israel, the Church would always be a mixed bag, yet the Lord remains with His people. Some have seen the reference to the scribe who brings forth new and old as a clue to the identity of the writer of Matthew's Gospel and a hint as to his purpose — to show Jesus as the fulfillment of everything Judaism was created to be. By the use of parables, the Lord illuminated what the disciples knew (the old) by His word (the new). We all come with differing perspectives and backgrounds to our community prayer. Like Matthew's scribe, we should let those experiences be illuminated by the Gospel message. We carry a great deal of material for our own parables which the Gospel can light up for us. Just as God adapted His presence to nomads and wanderers and then to a tribal league, an emergent nation and finally a population in exile, so Jesus remains with His Church through all its permutations and combinations until the end of time. Nobody has the power to rip the Church away from Jesus' side.

Point

Even in the complex mixture of the Church, there is always the opportunity for individual and community revival until the judgment.

FRIDAY — Seventeenth Week of the Year
Lv 23:1, 4-11, 15-16, 27, 34-37   *Mt 13:54-58*

First Reading

The first reading from the Book of Leviticus describes the holy days and seasons which God commanded the people to observe. These holy times were set aside not because God needed them but because the people did. Such times are vital to us as reminders of our religious identity. We set aside certain times and places to focus our attention on our relationship to God. Such sacred space is important because the successes, failures, problems, solutions and deals that make up the flow of our lives can cause us to forget another factor present through-out all our activities: God's Spirit slowly giving direction to this melange of events. We need prayer and space to distinguish that Spirit and His direction more clearly.

Gospel Reading

We need to focus God's Spirit in our lives because we can miss Him as did the people in Jesus' hometown. Their early enthusiasm became hobbled by doubt. They could not see the presence of God's Spirit in His words and deeds even though Jesus displayed great power elsewhere. The name for this is discernment. We live in a world filled with many lights and many voices. We need to take time to learn to discern that of the Spirit of God. This discernment is developed through prayer — those special times both private and liturgical that bind us together as a people and to the Lord. They give direc-tion and structure to our individual spiritual lives.

Point

Liturgical rites and seasons tie our personal spiritual struggles into the great drama of salvation history. They remind us that our successes and failures are part of the journey of God's people on earth.

SATURDAY — Seventeenth Week of the Year
Lv 25:1, 8-17   Mt 14:1-12

First Reading

The Book of Leviticus is really a civil, criminal and religious code all wrapped up in one. A careful reading reveals a wealth of information about Israelite life and culture. Today's first reading describes the Jubilee year to be held every fifty years. It is a model of our Catholic practice of the periodic Holy Year. The Jubilee year was a special time when all debts were canceled, slaves were freed and all property that had been sold or leased was returned to the owner. It remains a question whether the prescriptions for the Jubilee year were ever completely carried out or whether it was simply a social blueprint expressing an ideal wherein nobody should forever be a slave, be crushed by debt, or be obliged to sell the family farm without the possibility of redemption. It was a mechanism to give every person a chance for a fresh start with dignity. It was a device to prevent one human being from acquiring complete control over another person.

Gospel Reading

We see such power at work in today's Gospel reading in the story of the Baptist's death. We all know the circumstances of John's execution. Matthew places this incident after Jesus was rejected in His hometown to imply that a fate similar to that of John was now awaiting Jesus. We can see in the power that Herod had over people's lives the very evil that the Jubilee year was designed to prevent. We all have some degree of power over other people's lives. Our economic, psychological or legal leverage over others can take many forms. The question raised by these readings is whether we use such a position to enhance another person's dignity or not.

Point

Significantly, Jesus' opening sermon in Luke's Gospel in the Nazareth synagogue was a declaration of a spiritual Jubilee year. In the community Jesus founded, positions of power should not be used to keep people down, but to raise them up.

MONDAY — Eighteenth Week of the Year
Nb 11:4-15   Mt 14:13-21/Mt 14:22-36

First Reading

The traditions that are collected together in the Book of Numbers recount the wilderness phase of the Exodus story. It is called the Book of Numbers because it contains census lists and numbers. In this reading, the people become bored with the endless supply of manna and now hunger for meat with all the Egyptian delicacies they remember. Moses finally becomes exasperated by their constant drumbeat of complaint. The theological issue was not that they wanted meat instead of manna but that they looked exclusively to God for its provision. The slave mentality had pervaded their faith. They could not see God at work in their own initiative, intelligence and abilities.

Gospel Reading

The story from Numbers provides the background for today's Gospel reading. The people are in a deserted place and Jesus meets their hunger. Matthew is recounting much more than another miracle. Through this event, he shows that Jesus gives spiritual food that satisfies spiritual hunger. Indeed, in Jesus we have the fullness of spiritual life and through Him our physical hungers can be satisfied as well. This is a subtle but important point. We might reflect whether world hunger is the result of an inadequate food supply or inadequate distribution arrangements. Is the problem located in the sufficiency of our planet or the selfishness of the human heart? Should we expect God to deliver more food from heaven to feed the starving or to move human hearts to share what they have? God works through the secondary causes of human initiative, intelligence and concern. To mobilize our energies to alleviate human suffering requires the very change of heart that Jesus came to effect.

Point

To look at another human being as a brother or sister is the real miracle.

TUESDAY — Eighteenth Week of the Year
Nb 12:1-13   *Mt 14:22-36/Mt 15:1-2,10-14*

First Reading

A little bit of family jealousy is revealed in today's first reading. Miriam questions whether Moses is the exclusive vehicle for God's word to the people. The Lord responds that there would be times when He would speak through special prophets and extraordinary visions. However, ordinarily He would speak without fanfare or spectacular effects through Moses. Moses and his successors would be the routine intermediaries of God's leadership of His people. Miriam is warned, in effect, not to wait for clouds, thunder, lightning and visions. She should follow the established, institutional leadership which the Lord created. For her noisy antagonism, Miriam is turned into a leper — a seemingly disproportionate way of dealing with a vociferous layperson. Moses, of course, obtains remission of the penalty and things return to an unusually docile normality.

Gospel Reading

In this set of readings, Matthew deals particularly with the Church. The disciples in the boat traditionally represent the Church. In all the storms that rock our craft, Jesus is near. Peter is the disciple of bold initiative. As long as he kept his eye on Jesus and not on extraneous factors, he was safe. We might examine where we look for spiritual direction. We have certainly received the Holy Spirit. However, what certainty do we have that the movements we feel within are those of the Spirit? There are many things that claim to be of the Spirit. We can turn to the Church for navigation. The Lord gave us the Church as the ordinary guide for our spiritual growth. Occasionally, an extraordinary prophet arises to impel us in a neglected direction. But from year to year the Church is the ordinary channel of God's word to us without fanfare, lightning or thunder.

Point

It is by the Church that we can measure our enthusiasm, inspirations and excitements.

WEDNESDAY — Eighteenth Week of the Year
Nb 13:1-2, 25-14:1, 26-29, 34-35   Mt 15:21-28

First Reading

The Israelites are geographically close to the promised land but are psychologically very far away from it. Twelve spies are sent on a reconnaissance mission. Caleb returns with the recommendation that they go for it. The others remark in disagreement that the size of the towers looked ominous and the natives appeared to be "giants." On hearing this report, the people lament and wail into the night. They were waiting for God to intervene again. God does indeed intervene with a word of judgment that this generation will die in the desert. They were not yet ready for freedom. Here, in the desert, a new, tough generation will be raised who will be sure of the promise, certain that God chose them and secure in their national identity. They will be prepared to make bold moves in their confidence that the Lord is with them.

Gospel Reading

This episode of the Canaanite woman whose daughter was healed by Jesus is an early sign of the Church's mission to the Gentiles. Like the hesitation of the Israelites in today's first reading, the move to embrace non-Jews was not easily made by the early Church. Only when the first generation of Jewish Christians was dying out did the Gentile mission (as it was called) explode and then dominate the Church. These Greek Christians did not give the old Jewish connection a second thought. They were secure in their knowledge that the Spirit of the Lord was with them as they articulated the faith in Gentile terms. When a person is secure in his or her Catholic identity and aware of the presence of the Holy Spirit, such an individual can be bold in articulating the faith to every kind of audience.

We can all reach out very creatively and boldly when our home base is secure.

Point

If we are sure of our identity, we can be more bold in fashioning our apostolate and shaping our Christian life.

THURSDAY — Eighteenth Week of the Year
Nb 20:1-13   *Mt 16:13-23*

First Reading

In this first reading, the people are lacking water and again they turn to Moses. The Lord instructs Moses to command the rock to bring forth water. Instead, Moses strikes the rock twice. Water flows out but the Lord is displeased. Moses is then precluded from entering the promised land for this act of disobedience. The punishment seems to us to be excessively harsh. The Lord charges Moses with "not showing forth God's sanctity to the people." That can mean several things. It might refer to Moses' disobedience to God's command. It might indicate that he used his special position to berate the people. Perhaps it suggests the implied doubt Moses expressed in twice striking the rock, thus indicating that he shared more deeply in the people's lack of trust in God than he cared to acknowledge. Like the generation sentenced to remain in the desert, he would not see the promised land as a possession, only as a promise. A lesson we can draw from this episode is that while individual leaders do fail, our trust is in the Lord.

Gospel Reading

This is a famous section of Matthew's Gospel. It is one of several passages relating to Peter that illustrate the special position he held in the early Church. Jesus asks the disciples their judgment as to His identity. Their responses rerun the great figures of the Jewish past. Peter alone acknowledges Him as the promised Messiah. For that primal and foundational insight of faith, the Lord makes Peter the rock on which the Church will forever stand. The Catholic tradition refers this reading to the special place of Peter inherited by later Popes. The non-Catholic Christian tradition refers the Lord's words to the kind of faith Peter expressed. Both traditions agree that Peter's creed is the first stone of a durable building of which we are a part. Peter was given Sanhedrin-like authority to adapt the community Jesus founded to different generations and cultures. When the Lord speaks of coming suffering, the rock becomes a stumbling block. Even Peter had a great deal of learning to do.

Point

Even though we rightly hold religious leaders to a higher standard than others, our faith is always placed primarily in the Lord Jesus.

FRIDAY — Eighteenth Week of the Year
Dt 4:32-40   *Mt 16:24-28*

First Reading

The Book of Deuteronomy is built around the orations of Moses. A strict covenant theology from northern Israel was the core around which Deuteronomy took shape. It serves as an introduction to the history that will follow in Joshua, Judges, and First and Second Samuel and Kings. It seeks to express the mind of Moses as to the moral and spiritual significance of the Exodus and of the covenant. In this first reading, we have the words of Moses as he tries to drive home to the people and to future generations the drama of what has occurred. He asks whether any god has ever chosen a nation as God had chosen Israel. It is always fascinating to read about the immensity of outer space. It is boggling to try to realize that the light which reaches our bedrooms tonight from some distant galaxy began its journey millions of years before human beings existed on the earth. Yet, the power, energy and force that upholds all these stars is a Person who loves us. The Intelligence that drives the universe chose a wandering group of tribes as a people with sacramental significance for the human race.

Gospel Reading

God spoke through Moses and Jesus to us to enable us to fashion a spiritual life. Today, these scriptural readings are being heard in Japan, France, Nigeria and Brazil. In all of these places, people hear the words, "What profit . . ." These words resonate with them as they do with us because they speak to a universal human experience. We all can lose ourselves in events. We all play a variety of roles with family, friends and co-workers. By centering on Christ for a while, we can allow the Lord to become our Archimedean point of balance in a rapidly changing and often quixotic world.

Point

The God of the galaxies chose us in a special covenant so that His eternity can be our own.

SATURDAY — Eighteenth Week of the Year
Dt 6:4-13   *Mt 17:14-20*

First Reading

The opening prayer in today's reading, the *Shema,* is a declaration of Jewish faith. It is sung at every synagogue service in the world. It is Deuteronomy's call for wholehearted, sincere love of God and an exhortation to more than merely external observance. It is the soul of Old Testament faith quoted by Jesus in His own time of desert temptation and to the Jews when they asked Him about the greatest commandment. This call to a deep love of God is predicated on the great act God had performed in bringing the people to the promised land. They are poised on the edge of a land filled with abundance. The long wilderness wandering is over. This moment, the reason for loving God, was to be the sign of God's love for His people through the generations.

Gospel Reading

In a controlled liturgical aside, Matthew has the epileptic's father say to Jesus, in Greek, *Kyrie eleison,* "Lord, have mercy." Jesus responds with a call for deephearted faith. The faith that can move mountains is more than intellectual assent. It is trust in God. This confidence is filled with the certainty that God will protect the innermost part of ourselves and that our deepest core is safe in His hands. A life of such total trust can do wondrous things and achieve great results in others. This is the reason the Lord's words are coupled with an exorcism that only He could perform. The lesson Matthew teaches is that we can exorcise demons of every sort from our lives and the environment around us if our faith is deep, secure and abiding.

Point

Powerful and deep trust in God is never without public effect.

MONDAY — Nineteenth Week of the Year
Dt 10:12-22   *Mt 17:22-27*

First Reading

The Book of Deuteronomy speaks in exalted liturgical tones of Israel's God. People become like the God they worship. If our God is one of vengeance, reprisal and scrupulosity, those will become our traits. For this reason, Moses emphasizes in these closing words to his people that this God is one of generosity, kindness and impartiality, befriending widow and orphan. The people are told to circumcise their hearts, that is, to perform radical surgery on their souls and minds and come to see that they are to show the same kindness to others that God has shown to them. They are to forgive as God has forgiven them. We can see this ancient tradition brought back to life in the teaching of Jesus. The recital of these words of Deuteronomy would remind people of their loyalty to the God of the Exodus as they enter a pagan land.

Gospel Reading

The issue of the Temple tax arises. The Temple was an expensive place to run. This Jewish version of the *cathedraticum* enabled the priests to rely on something more than the fluctuating free-will offerings of those who visited the Temple. The reason Matthew recounts this story is interesting. By the time Matthew wrote his Gospel, the Temple had been destroyed by the Romans a few years earlier. Yet, although the Temple was gone, predictably enough the Temple tax remained. Matthew recalls these words of the Lord to encourage the Jewish Christians to be aware of the sensitivities of others. Although they no longer had a moral obligation to pay the tax, they should have enough respect for their ancestral heritage to do so if they could. The range of our spiritual responsibilities is wider than those embodied in civil or religious law.

Point

The Spirit leads us beyond strict legal obligation to a wider world of sensitive concern.

TUESDAY — Nineteenth Week of the Year
Dt 31:1-8   *Mt 18:1-5, 10, 12-14*

First Reading

This first reading recounts the passage of authority from Moses to Joshua. It signaled the need for a different type of leadership since Israel was now on the offense. This section comes at the conclusion of the Book of Deuteronomy, a long reflection on the covenant. It presents a stark covenant theology: Israel was chosen as a people. The land was theirs not by national right but as a gift. If they kept the covenant, they would prosper. If they broke the covenant, God would take the land from them either in bits and pieces or wholesale. The books of Joshua through Second Kings will show this principle at work with the precision of a micrometer. This entire collection, called the Deuteronomic history, is a theological account that looks beneath all the economic, social and political reasons for Israel's fortunes to highlight fidelity or infidelity to God as the motor force of her history. It functions as a national examination of conscience that reviews the past in the light of the covenant. Put into final form during a time of religious revival in Judah after the northern tribes had been exiled, the Deuteronomic history is a retrospective on Israel's turbulent and sad history in the light of faith.

Gospel Reading

Today's Gospel reading is also about self-examination. It speaks to the internal life of the Church in any age. Jesus instructs His disciples and us not to be preoccupied with ranking ourselves but with serving the rest. It is the person willing to occupy the child's place at the bottom of the ladder who will prove to be most important in the spiritual life of the kingdom. When the Lord speaks of straying sheep, the emphasis is not only on the joy of finding the lost sheep as in Luke's Gospel. It is also put on the duty of the bishop, pastor or fellow-Christian to seek out those who have fallen away and not simply to wait for the wanderers to make an appointment to seek readmission.

Point

There are many ways to improve parish life. But the light of Christ shines most clearly in our covenant faithfulness to the Lord.

WEDNESDAY — Nineteenth Week of the Year
Dt 34:1-12   *Mt 18:15-20*

First Reading

As Moses comes to the end of his life, he is allowed to glimpse the promised land and to view the goal of the journey. Very often, we feel like Moses. All of us work for a better society and for the growth of a Christian community. We know that we will not see that promised land. Now and then, however, the Lord allows us a glimpse of what the future will be like so that we can see with our eyes the concrete goal toward which we are working. We know that others will enjoy the full fruit of our labor. This is very close to the heart of what it means to be a community. All of us spend ourselves working to enhance and hasten the appearance of the reign of God on earth. Just as we are heirs of the missionary efforts of generations before us, so those who follow us will receive the results of what we have done. Our efforts are not, therefore, in vain. They all come together into a future that we can only imagine. There will be no tomb for Moses to become a tourist attraction. His monument is Judaism.

Gospel Reading

This elaborate procedure of reconciliation does not sound like the historical Jesus we know. In fact, it sounds much like a procedure devised by a church committee. Very probably, that is exactly what it is. In Matthew's church, a certain stability or organization had been achieved and this structured way of dealing with conflict was developed and seen as the Lord's will as to how controversies should be resolved. The original impulse of Jesus was to forgive until it hurts. The second part of this reading is closer to Jesus' words. Where two or three Christians are gathered in Jesus' name in judgment, prayer, decision-making, reconciliation, conversation or planning, He will be there. The sense of this entire passage is not to tolerate breaches in the local church community. The healing process is vital and not to be delayed. Expulsion or suspension is only to be a last resort.

Point

When conflict arises, there is a Christian way of conflict management.

THURSDAY — Nineteenth Week of the Year

Jos 3:7-10, 11, 13-17   *Mt 18:21-19:1*

First Reading

Joshua (the Hebrew form of the name "Jesus") now as-sumes command of the people. Moses was a hard act to follow but Joshua did not hesitate. In this liturgical account of the solemn entry into the promised land, Joshua instructs the priests to carry the ark across the Jordan. The waters make way in an event reminiscent of the Red Sea crossing. Once in the promised land, Joshua will impose circumcision upon everyone born in the desert and then begin the conquest. The Canaanites did not easily step aside (much as the American Indians did not easily let the European newcomers invade). What followed was a savage, "holy" war with a great deal of butchery on both sides. The Book of Joshua recounts this conquest in an Israelite version of "How the West Was Won."

Gospel Reading

Even after twenty centuries, we are startled at the refusal of the servant whose mammoth debt was forgiven to delay the repayment of a trifling sum owed to him. The teaching of this Gospel parable is a contrast with today's first reading. We are to forgive seventy times seven, that is, we are not to keep count. Some early Christian non-conformists used to say that the Old and New Testaments portray two different Gods: one of bloodthirsty revenge and the other of love. Actually, the con-trast is not so stark. The Old Testament does speak of love, befriending the alien and caring for the needy. The New Testa-ment does speak of judgment and the coming return of the Lord, as at the conclusion of today's parable. There remains a difference between Testaments that reflects a growing change in our human understanding of God. The Old Testament, a story of religious consciousness periodically lurched forward by God's revelation of Himself, recounts mankind's evolving view of God: God as warrior, king, shepherd. Even in the New Testament, we have the Church's gradual appreciation of the nature of Jesus — His ministry, Resurrection and words about the Father.

Point

The Old Testament is replete with avenging justice. Jesus came to show us that human relations were to be governed by self-sacrificing love.

FRIDAY — Nineteenth Week of the Year
Jos 24:1-13   *Mt 19:3-12*

First Reading

This is an extremely important chapter from the Book of Joshua. It recounts a ceremony of covenant renewal for the league of tribes at Shechem, an important tribal center before David made Jerusalem Israel's capital. The tribal leaders gathered there periodically to renew their covenant. When they did so, they recalled the story of what God had done for them as Joshua does in today's reading. It is a religious recounting that views everything from the standpoint of the covenant. Because it was a ceremony of renewal, increasingly more of their recent past was drawn into the covenant story as time passed. As their history became more complex, this ceremony became an opportunity to return to first principles. Our covenant renewal is the eucharistic celebration when we review our personal story with the eye of faith and return to first principles.

Gospel Reading

The Pharisees seek to draw Jesus into a rabbinic debate

about the enabling conditions of divorce. The Lord points back to a Genesis time when there was no divorce at all. That look back brings us to first principles in regard to the marriage covenant. Especially in a world which views marriage as the stuff of media humor, the contrast between the condition of marriage today and the vision of Genesis is stark and sad. It shows us how far we have departed from first principles. Both Genesis and the Gospels demonstrate to us how quickly our culture is spinning from the center in eccentric, centrifugal fashion. Our regular celebration of the Eucharist reminds us of the centripetal truths to which we have dedicated our lives.

Point

The Eucharistic celebration brings the Holy Thursday moment into the present. In the middle of our joys and sorrows we say again: Amen! You are Lord!

SATURDAY — Nineteenth Week of the Year
Jos 24:14-29   *Mt 19:13-15*

First Reading

Today's first reading describes the creation of a confederation or league of tribes. Another era ends with Joshua's death. After him, there will be no single leader for a while but a series of occasional, charismatic judges. Two things deserve note about today's reading. At the periodic renewal of the covenant, the saving deeds of God were recited. This recital became the group memory and the core of the Torah. Later, national and regional traditions would be collected around this spine. For that reason, these oldest sections sound liturgical and publicly recitable. Secondly, the covenant was regularly renewed so that both each subsequent generation and new worshippers of Israel's God could affirm for themselves this ancient act of faith.

At times, the local inhabitants or various immigrants converted to belief in the God of Israel. By this renewal ceremony, they assimilated themselves into the covenant story. It is similar to naturalized citizens who assume as their own the conventional history of the United States. By choosing the God of Israel, they became part of the covenant people and a conscious part of God's saving plan.

Gospel Reading

Some writers see in this incident the result of a discussion in the early Church on the place of children in the community. This scene of Jesus and the children shows Him inviting those of least consequence and with no powerful standing to Himself. Even though we might feel inferior to everyone else, we are worth a million in the Lord's sight.

Point

To the extent that we accept the Lord's call to us, we become a more conscious and articulate part of God's saving design for all people.

MONDAY — Twentieth Week of the Year
Jg 2:11-19   *Mt 19:16-22*

First Reading

The judges were charismatic, military leaders. Some of their names are familiar to us: Samuel, Gideon, Deborah, Samson. Today's first reading continues the theme of the Deuteronomic history. When the people disobeyed the Commandments, disaster befell them. They would then follow a judge who would deliver them from the enemy. The connection between obedience to the Commandments and prosperity was not an arbitrary one. The Commandments put into words the basic rules of civility. They forbid theft, murder, adultery, perjury. When these rules are disregarded, the result, in any time or place, is chaos as was rampant in the time of the judges. The Commandments are not specially Christian. They are the basic rules of civilized society.

Gospel Reading

Today's reading speaks about spiritual growth. Spiritual development in a Christian direction begins when we go beyond the Commandments. The rich man steps from the crowd and asks Jesus for the path to a deeper, more fulfilling spirituality. The Commandments were a way of life for him. He wanted more. The Lord tells him to make an affirmative decision, to break with the crowd, to leave all he has and to follow. The young man could not do this. Our relationship with the Lord is like any other relationship. The more time we spend with someone, our conversation becomes easier, and the relationship more intimate, rewarding and profound. For such an individual we are willing to do much more, to go out of our way and even be heroic. But, if we meet someone only once or twice a year at Christmas or Easter, the conversation is formal, stilted and strained. A marvelous description of the mature spiritual life is "the practice of the presence of God." We enter that world of spiritual growth when we move beyond the Commandments.

Point

The Commandments provide the baseline from which Christian spiritual growth begins.

TUESDAY — Twentieth Week of the Year
Jg 6:11-24   *Mt 19:23-30*

First Reading

After Joshua died, only a loose confederation of tribes remained, without any central authority. These judges were popular leaders like our Paul Bunyan or Davy Crockett. They were not necessarily saints but heroes who rose to deliver the people from a particular peril. The Book of Judges recounts the stories of twelve of them. Today's first reading is about Gideon. The peril facing Israel was the Midianites. They were nomads who came on the crest of an innovation called "camel-riding" — a primitive kind of blitzkrieg. Gideon formed an army that God eventually whittled down to 300 men. It numbered so few to make it plain that victory was from the Lord. Gideon used a ruse of noise and lights to create the impression of a much larger army. The Midianites fled in fear as this victory went down in Israelite memory as the "Day of Midian." The message of the story is the need for reliance on the power of God operative through us.

Gospel Reading

The rich man refused to give everything up to follow the Lord. Jesus remarks on the difficulty faced by those with property in entering the reign of God. This was paradoxical to the disciples. For them, prosperity was a sign of God's blessing. If the rich, so obviously blessed, could not enter the kingdom, then the chances of everyone else were dismal indeed. The effect would be similar to the Lord's assertion of the difficulty the healthy have to enter the kingdom. Those wracked with pain would react as did the disciples. If we structure our life around property, then as long as life continues without event, all may be well. But when we face the challenge of evil or personal chaos, we stagger because the items with which we surround ourselves cannot deliver inner strength.

Point

Real strength is not financial or physical but spiritual. The Lord alone can give us inner substance and vision.

WEDNESDAY — Twentieth Week of the Year
Jg 9:6-15   Mt 20:1-16

First Reading

The story of Abimelech is the center of the Book of Judges. He was Gideon's illegitimate son, actually one of seventy sons. Abimelech hired riffraff ("worthless loafers" as the Bible calls them) as a private army. He then assassinated all his brothers except the youngest, Jotham, who escaped. The people made Abimelech leader or quasi-king. Later, Jotham delivers this parable about plants. The best plants had no time to be king. But the buckthorn, a repulsive bush because it was useless (it provided no shade) and dangerous (it was combustible), agreed to be king. Jotham's point is that kings are either useless or dangerous. After reciting this trenchant little homily, like Patrick Henry, he ran out of town. Abimelech was a brutal and ruthless man. After three years, the people rebelled. He burned many of them alive and he himself finally died violently. The lesson the Book of Judges derives from this is: "Thus did God requite the evil Abimelech had done in killing his seventy brothers." He got what was coming to him. The logic of Deuteronomy is relentless. Only God is king.

Gospel Reading

Today's reading is about people getting what is coming to

them. The late workers were paid as much as the early ones. The point of the parable is that they were paid not because of the amount of time they worked but because they answered the call. When we apply this to ourselves, we come to appreciate the fact that God does not compare us with other people such as Francis of Assisi or Teresa of Avila. The Lord looks at what we have done with what we have. He examines how we have used the opportunities and skills we have been given. Each of us in this way writes his or her own unique spiritual story. Abimelech wrote his. We write ours.

Point

We fashion our own spiritual life or spiritual death.

THURSDAY — Twentieth Week of the Year
Jg 11:29-39   *Mt 22:1-14*

First Reading

The last judge we will consider is Jephthah in his fight with the Ammonites. With all the Midianites, Moabites, Canaanites, Philistines and Ammonites around, we can wonder how thorough was the conquest that Joshua had proclaimed. Jephthah was a roving warlord who was commissioned by several tribes to do battle with the Ammonite enemy. The tribe of Ephraim was angry because Jephthah had not included them in the war party or the division of spoils. They sent a punitive expedition against him. To uncover the Ephraimites among his army, Jephthah had all strangers pronounce the word *Shibboleth,* a test word that would reveal an Ephraimite accent. Those who failed the test were summarily executed. Today's first reading takes place before the Ammonite defeat. Jephthah vowed that if he was given victory, he would sacrifice the first thing that came through his door. He won the victory and the first thing to enter his house was his daughter. He kept the vow. This is a savage story typical of a brutal time. The judges were not saints but military heroes. The "vow" Jephthah made was the product of an evolving faith struggling out of Canaanite ways. It reminds us that the chosen people did not drop out of heaven ready-made. They were the result of a long process of which the various episodes in the Book of Judges are snapshots.

Gospel Reading

Jesus delivers the parable of the banquet, the invitees' refusal and the search among the slums for new guests. The major reference is to the Jewish refusal of God's call to them in Jesus. That refusal took various historical forms, some of which we were able to glimpse in the Book of Judges. The parable's second part describing the lack of a proper garment reminds us who have accepted the call that not everyone can enter the kingdom. We must come prepared to celebrate. We should examine the kind of life and love we bring to this Eucharist and whether we have come here prepared for transformation of all we have and are by the Lord.

Point

How we are "dressed" — what we bring to the liturgy — is important for a eucharistic effect on our lives.

FRIDAY — Twentieth Week of the Year
Rt 1:1, 3-6, 14-16, 22   *Mt 22:34-40*

First Reading

The story of Ruth is a special story. It is not just about a woman's love for her husband but for another woman as well — her mother-in-law. Naomi traveled with her husband and two sons to Moab where they married pagan women. Later, her husband and sons died. Naomi was left with her two daughters-in-law. She decided to return home and instructed her two daughters-in-law to do likewise. One returned to her own people but Ruth did not. She told Naomi, "Wherever you go, I will go . . . your God will be my God too." She remained with the older woman. This quiet, gentle story is a refreshing aside during this savage period of the judges. While armies were slugging it out in the majestic and bloody movement of salvation history, here, in this warm and simple relationship between Ruth and Naomi, God's plan is also unfolding.

Gospel Reading

What is striking about Jesus' response in today's Gospel reading is not the command to love God and to love neighbor but that He joined them as two sides of the same coin. Love of God and of neighbor are not artificially connected. If a person really loves his or her neighbor (as Ruth did Naomi) such a person loves God (by whatever name they know Him.) After all, Ruth was not Jewish but nevertheless very much a spiritual daughter of Abraham.

Point

Alongside councils, encyclicals and Papal elections, the deep warm relationships of our lives have a place in the salvation of the world.

SATURDAY — Twentieth Week of the Year
Rt 2:1-3, 8-11; 4:13-17   *Mt 23:1-12*

First Reading

Ruth returned to her mother-in-law's hometown of Bethlehem after the death of her husband. One day, while Ruth was picking grain, she met the plantation owner named Boaz.

Eventually they married. They had a son named Obed who was the father of Jesse and the grandfather of David, an ancestor of Jesus. We should note that not once in this entire story of Ruth's affectionate relationship to Naomi or Boaz is the word "love" mentioned. Yet that is exactly what the entire book is about. The writer did not have to use the word because it was exemplified in Ruth's life. Historians might not consider the Book of Ruth significant but the Bible, which tells a larger story than secular history, places this humble Gentile girl among its heroines. This is especially true for us Christians because generations after Ruth, in Bethlehem, the love of Ruth and Boaz glowed once more in the soul of Jesus.

Gospel Reading

The message of Jesus to us is that we keep God's Word without panoply and fanfare. It is not title and position but humble receptivity to the Word of God that marks out the true believers and followers of the Lord. Ruth's unassuming love and care for others marks her as an ancestor of Jesus in ways more than biological. Although she was a Gentile, she was very much an "anonymous Israelite" and keeper of the Law. It is the attitude of heart that makes us children of God in the deepest and most enduring sense.

Point

Openness to God's Word links individuals throughout the generations as people of God and as brothers and sisters in the Lord.

MONDAY — Twenty-First Week of the Year
1 Th 1:2-5, 8-10   *Mt 23:13-22*

First Reading

The Thessalonian letters are important because they are

the oldest parts of the New Testament we have and the earliest of Paul's letters. We see in them young Christian congregations about twenty years after the Lord's Resurrection struggling to live the Christian faith. Paul sent this letter to encourage them to keep faith especially in the light of the immediately expected return of the Lord. It is in the light of the anticipated quick return of Jesus that these letters should be read. Today's introduction emphasizes the uncomplicated faith of the Thessalonians. It is a faith and a life lived for Jesus who is to deliver them from the wrath to come.

Gospel Reading

We can compare the simple faith of the Thessalonians with today's Gospel reading. It is a strong denunciation of Pharisees and Pharisaism. It seems as though this is a different Jesus from the One to whom we are accustomed. There is a sharp change in tone as He lashes out at some of these religious leaders who slammed shut the door to God, corrupted converts and played casuistic games with sacred oaths. Of course, there was nothing vicious about the Law, Covenant and Old Testament theology. It was what these leaders did with these sacred realities that excites the Lord's anger. His condemnation of Pharisaism is really a critique of the excesses of religion in any culture. Religion at its best can enhance communion with God and convey to individuals personal strength and a full spiritual life. At its worst, religion can be made to harry people with obligations and obsess them with guilt. Jesus came to heal and restore not only individuals but the good name of religion.

Point

When religion becomes complicated, it is useful to look to the faith of the early Christians and the manner in which they saw Christ — as One who delivers from the wrath to come.

TUESDAY — Twenty-First Week of the Year
1 Th 2:1-8   *Mt 23:23-26*

First Reading

In this first reading, Paul speaks about his manner of teaching. He did not use flattery or come with self-serving motives as did the religious entrepreneurs who made their way throughout the region. In an early Christian document called the *Didache,* people are warned to let wandering preachers reside with them only one or two days. If they remain longer than that, they are becoming parasitical and can be regarded as false teachers. Paul is anxious to distinguish himself from these promoters. He was as gentle as a nursing mother. The real function of a priest or teacher is not to pump people full of information and grace but to assist them to spiritual maturity. Philosophers often speak of the Socratic method, a technique designed to elicit truth from students. Socrates used to call himself a midwife in his enabling students to realize their capacity for truth and judgment. We all have the ability to recognize truth within us. A teacher's function is to activate that capacity. The religious teacher is an enabler and not a religious encyclopedia. The function of an apostle, priest or religious teacher is to assist the growth of mature individuals in the Lord.

Gospel Reading

A lack of spiritual maturity dominates today's Gospel reading. We are in the presence of classic instances of missing the point. The Pharisees engaged in excessive tithing while overlooking the more significant requirements of basic justice and mercy. They strained out the unclean gnat but swallowed the camel. They were preoccupied with the outward appearance of the cup without a second thought for its insides. Spiritual maturity frequently comes to a matter of priorities. The difference between a child and an adult is not found simply in the quantity of information received and retained but in the manner in which that information is processed and ordered. The adult presumably knows what is important and what is not. Spiritual maturity is also a matter of evaluation. Some religious regulations are more important than others.

Point

Maturity cannot be taught. It is a gift toward which a good leader helps us grow.

WEDNESDAY — Twenty-First Week of the Year
1 Th 2:9-13   *Mt 23:27-32*

First Reading

Paul further underscores the authenticity of his ministry among the Thessalonians by referring to his life style. It was not only what he taught but the way he lived that provided corroboration of the Gospel he preached. His constant encouragement and comfort to them was meant to incarnate Jesus Christ. The Thessalonians received his words in the proper spirit and treated Paul's message not simply as another evangelical approach but as the Gospel of God. How we live our lives and treat fellow-believers gives added clout and credibility to the words we speak. The power of the Gospel is not an independent entity that magically attracts listeners as though the lives of its adherents were irrelevant to its truth. What people see transpiring in parishes and Catholic families lends believability to the Gospel message.

Gospel Reading

Jesus' condemnation of Pharisaism continues apace. Their

hypocrisy brought disrepute upon the holy realities of Law, Temple and Covenant. They gave religion a bad name. He pronounces the judgment that they will have to pay for centuries of disregard of the prophets by their forebears. The years of abuse of the covenant were about to terminate. A new covenant is taking place that will replace the energy and power of the old that had been dissipated by centuries of manipulation and mechanization. As the Pharisees stand to the side unrepentant, God is making new arrangements to reveal and share His life with people.

Point

How people live their faith reveals the truth of that faith to others.

THURSDAY — Twenty-First Week of the Year
1 Th 3:7-13   *Mt 24:42-51*

First Reading

Paul points to a truth in today's first reading that we have all often felt but to which we may not have paid much attention. He tells the Thessalonians that he has been consoled by their faith to such a degree that he thrives only if they stand firm. Our faith has its mountains and valleys. Belonging to a community of faith assists us in the valleys. When we tend to drift or settle into a spiritual "neutral," the sight of others in prayer, faithfully celebrating the Eucharist gives us strength to pass through the valley back to the plain. This is one important rationale for belonging to a parish community. Left to ourselves, we can develop a highly one-sided, even oddball spirituality. By inclusion in a parish that encompasses a wide spectrum of spiritual vitalities, we tend to balance ourselves.

Gospel Reading

Jesus describes the faithful far-sighted servant who is vigilant although he does not know the exact moment of his master's return. The Lord speaks directly to Church leaders of any era who might forget that they are temporarily standing in His place. They represent but do not replace the Lord. He speaks as well to all of us who might forget the goal for which we are working. The problem addressed here is not drift but shortsightedness which sees short-run success or failure as final, while forgetting our place in the larger design of the Lord. In the Christian tradition, spiritual life flourishes best in communal settings. We are called to collective light, life and communion. The parish community reminds us that we all participate in a drama much larger than the individual scenes of our own life.

Point

The community of faith is important to help us keep perspective and avoid spiritual drift.

FRIDAY — Twenty-First Week of the Year
1 Th 4:1-8   *Mt 25:1-13*

First Reading

Paul exhorts the Thessalonians to grow in holiness and to abstain from sexual and financial immorality because the Lord is an avenger. Yet, at the beginning of this letter, he speaks of the Lord as One who delivers us from wrath. The two statements can be reconciled. Some theologians say there comes a point when we make a final choice for or against God. It happens at the moment of death in the last flicker of consciousness. Everything in our life to that point — the decisions, prayers, good done or left undone — all of it prepares us for and is poured into that climactic second. That instant pulls together all we have done and become and expresses itself as a final act of faith or mortal defiance of God. Before that moment, however, is the time for forgiveness, conversion, reparation, faith, hope and growth in the Lord.

Gospel Reading

The finality of death is one meaning of the Gospel parable of the ten virgins. Originally, its reference was to the Jews who were unprepared for the Messiah's coming as well as to Christians unprepared for the Second Coming. It applies, as well, to all of us. The delay in the parable was caused by the groom's haggling with the bride's family over the dowry arrangements. Meanwhile, some attendants ran out of oil. At the groom's return, those with oil do not share it — an unusual accent in a parable. Yet, there comes a final moment when there is no longer time to share. Certain things cannot be done at the last minute. We can recite many things on our deathbed but there is a great inertia dragging on our attitudes that we cannot instantly change. In the end, we face the Lord not with fine words recited in the fear of death but with the kind of person we have become. The point of this parable is not to inflict terror on anyone but to comfort those who have spent their lives in faithful adherence to Gospel living as best they could.

Point

We should not be paralyzed by the thought of our death. All the things we have done in our life add up. They determine cumulatively whether we will see the Lord as Avenger or saving Brother.

SATURDAY — Twenty-First Week of the Year
1 Th 4:9-12   Mt 25:14-30

First Reading

Paul makes a final exhortation in this first half of the Thessalonian letter that these Christians continue to love each other. He implies, and we know, that Christian love is in part the result of human effort but is also a gift from God. The medievals called it an infused virtue or power that we receive in baptism. This inner Spirit urges us toward deeper love. Paul asks them to be careful of their public conduct. At this early stage of the Church's existence, the behavior of Christians was closely watched not only for legal reasons but also for evidence of what these unconventional doctrines were really like. This is the reason for Paul's advice to remain at peace with each other, to work diligently and to give good example to outsiders. This was more than a spiritual aside — it was an invitation to an apostolic way of life that would win adherents.

Gospel Reading

This parable of the talents, both exploited and unused, speaks on several levels to us. We can apply Jesus' story not only to the spiritual gifts we have received but also to the intellectual and material opportunities we have been given. It is our obligation to use all we have in the service of the Lord. That does not require that we transfer title of everything we own to the Church. It does mean that we use our social opportunities and business contacts as ways of enhancing the rule of the Lord on earth. Gifts used in that way are multiplied and lead to greater opportunity. Gifts that are unused simply remain unused. We are all responsible to the Lord for everything we have been given. Through its members, the Church has received an enormous abundance of gifts for the spread of the Gospel. Too often a fearful attitude that seeks only to preserve the past and not to launch out into the future has hindered the growth of the Gospel.

Point

How we live in the world, as well as how we pray in church, can be apostolic and powerfully evangelistic.

MONDAY — Twenty-Second Week of the Year
1 Th 4:13-18   *Lk 4:16-18*

First Reading

Another issue that troubled the Thessalonian Church was that of the specific details of the Lord's second coming. They were concerned whether those of their number who had died would be incorporated into the coming kingdom of God on earth. Paul asserts in response that those who are living will have no advantage over those who have passed away because those who have died will rise on the last day. The spiritual bonds that link us with one another and with Jesus are deathless. It is important that we not become too materialistic in our discussion of the resurrection on the last day. Too excessive a preoccupation with the mechanics of shifting protons and neutrons to reintegrate the bodies of those who have died long ago can devaluate the deep significance of this mystery of faith. Paul's central point is that whole persons, not shades or spooks, shall live with the Lord; the spiritual unity we know as baptized brothers and sisters will continue forever.

Gospel Reading

Jesus comes to His home town after His return from the desert and speaks in the Nazareth synagogue for the first time.

He reads an ancient prophecy from Isaiah of Babylon describing the era of the Messiah. He then startles the audience by proclaiming that here, in Nazareth, this revered old prophecy is coming true in their sight. The future has begun. The resulting shock was tremendous. Amid the people's wonderment was also the question of how one they knew so well could be the person of such promised magnitude. The Lord articulates a typically Lukan theme of the reach of God's favor beyond intramural Judaism. A pagan widow and a Gentile official called Naaman in the Old Testament were cured and shown favor by God. This appeal to conveniently forgotten precedents caused the congregation to eject Him from the synagogue. At the start of His ministry in Luke's Gospel, the Lord states that the scope of the kingdom is worldwide and not limited to any one group. With all the differences we create among ourselves, the spiritual links of our truest humanity cross boundaries and synthetic separations.

Point

Invisible spiritual bonds are more lasting than the artificial differences we create.

TUESDAY — Twenty-Second Week of the Year
1 Th 5:1-6, 9-11   *Lk 4:31-37*

First Reading

As we come to the end of Paul's letter to the Thessalonians, this reading is itself about the end. People were very much aware of the coming end of the age but did not know the exact moment of its arrival. It was a feeling similar to that on the eve of World War II when everyone knew that war was coming but did not know its precise moment. Paul advises the Thessalonians not to let this uncertainty paralyze them. In our own time, there is a great deal of speculation about the end of the world.

The Catholic tradition has more frequently emphasized the end less as a cosmic affair than as the moment of our death when all the things on which we have depended will be withdrawn. Our faith enables us to see that the strength and life which last come from the Lord. Paul insists that preoccupation with the end of the world can quite literally drive a person crazy. However, awareness of the fragility of things will enable us to live more fully in the power of the Resurrection.

Gospel Reading

As we start Luke's Gospel, the first exorcism occurs in a place of worship. The "unclean spirit" can mean several things. Whether it was natural or supernatural, Jesus' power over it is undeniable. In this simple and direct sign of the Lord's power, we have a microscopic view of Christ's final victory. To people haunted by demons, the message of this passage is of the Lord's abiding power over our modern demons as well. We continue to await that final manifestation of Jesus' Easter victory for all to see as it permeates our world. Our faith tells us that it is just a matter of time. There came a point in World War II when the Allies knew they had won. The rest of the war simply made that victory clear.

Point

The power of the Lord's victory over all kinds of unclean spirits belongs to us through Baptism. It is called grace.

WEDNESDAY — Twenty-Second Week of the Year
Col 1:1-8   *Lk 4:38-44*

First Reading

We begin Paul's letter to the Colossians. Oddly, this dynamic little letter, one of the greatest Paul ever wrote, is written to one of the smallest Christian communities. Its theme is the cosmic Christ in whom is the fullness of life. In today's first reading, he refers to the Gospel they have heard and continue to live. Jesus never wrote a word nor did He instruct His disciples to write anything. They were sent to preach His word. As long as the eyewitnesses to what Jesus had done were around, there was no problem. As they died, there was a need to commit the cherished traditions that had grown about the Lord into writing. Thus, we have the Scriptures. It is important to realize at this early stage that the Gospel to which Paul refers is a living tradition — preached, lived, remembered, celebrated but probably not yet recorded. In the same way, the living tradition that continues in the Church today is also able to give life.

Gospel Reading

The insistence of Jesus that He and His disciples move to other towns to announce the message of the kingdom does not depreciate the healing ministry that He always continued. The healing ministry was the word in action. It was important to the Lord that the word of life be widely known and lived. The preaching was initially one of repentance and the covenant presence of the rule of God in people's lives. The realization of this message in act, structure and organization was to be also a healing ministry.

Point

To continue the ministry of Christ is not simply to repeat His words but to communicate and exhibit the Word as He did.

THURSDAY — Twenty-Second Week of the Year
Col 1:9-14   *Lk 5:1-11*

First Reading

The people at Colossae were troubled by a syncretistic mixing of Christianity with astrology and gnosticism. There were all kinds of strange infiltrations into their faith along with bits and pieces of Judaism. Paul writes to them about the centrality and sufficiency of belief in Jesus. In today's first reading, he reminds his readers that God has rescued us from the powers of darkness and brought us into the kingdom of His Son. Paul then prays that they may come to know God's will for them through spiritual insight. One way we can seek that insight is through the reading of Scripture. When we read it prayerfully and slowly (in a good translation), we notice that the same passage at different times in our life projects different meanings to us. That is one meaning of inspiration. When we read the Word of God, we know that it is the Holy Spirit speaking to us.

Gospel Reading

Another aid to spiritual insight is found in today's Gospel reading. The call of Simon to be a fisher of men (and women) reminds us that the Church was created by Jesus to help us attain perfect wisdom and spiritual sight. If the teaching of the Church is so pivotal, we should seek ready access to it through the documents of the Vatican Council — especially the Decree on Divine Revelation. Modern and classic spiritual writers and modern lives of the saints are important vehicles for spiritual reality testing. Through them, we develop spiritual insight by bouncing our experience off the masters. After our baptism, we are not dropped into the kingdom without further resources. We have the Scriptures and the traditions of the Church, as well as the great spiritual writers. They all enable us not to be content with spiritual mediocrity but to push out into deeper waters.

Point

Christian tradition helps us grow in the knowledge and love of the Lord.

FRIDAY — Twenty-Second Week of the Year
Col 1:15-20   *Lk 5:33-39*

First Reading

This magnificent passage from Colossians is a great hymn to Christ. A problem that plagued the Colossians was the belief in and recourse to the spirit world. Paul asserts that Jesus is supreme over things visible and invisible. He is the first-born, that is, the beginning of the new creation in which many will come to share. John's Gospel begins its prologue: "In the beginning was the Word. . ." It proclaims the mystery of the Incarnation. Here, Paul proclaims the mystery of salvation with Jesus on the Cross, "reconciling everything . . . making peace through (His) blood." These two mysteries provide the bases for the two great theologies of the Church: of the Incarnation and of the Redemption. Jesus — true God and true man — through His death and Resurrection is "head of the Church," the source of its authority and life. The power of Jesus is channeled to us through the community He founded. Sacramental power is not a free-floating energy; it derives from the very life of Jesus Himself.

Gospel Reading

The Lord speaks about new wine and new wineskins. Christianity is more than a new set of parables, new teachings or a new way of putting old things together. We should not force a similarity between Jesus and Judaism that is not there. We have in Christ a new power for human beings. In Jesus, we have the start of a new creation — a humanity that can reach God, know God and live the life of God through a supernatural source of life. In the present age, we have to labor, fast and strive to draw fully from that source of life.

Point

Christianity is more than old religious principles wrapped in new practices. In Jesus, a new meaning and purpose of creation are summed up. He is what we are all meant to be.

SATURDAY — Twenty-Second Week of the Year
Col 1:21-23   *Lk 6:1-5*

First Reading

The reconciliation Jesus achieved with God was not an abstract or atemporal event. It took place in His body, in a particular place and at a particular time to which we can point as the precise moment when mankind was put at peace with the Father. We make that reconciliation ours by linking ourselves with Jesus through a life and prayer like His own. This is one reason why Gospel preaching is vital. The great reunion with God that the Lord effected on Calvary and at Easter is ours when we assimilate ourselves to Him. That is the process through which this key event of salvation enters our lives. Our reconciliation with God is also not an abstract or merely logical thing. It is a real world occurrence that we must live out and put into practice.

Gospel Reading

The institution of the Sabbath is the occasion for Jesus to

make a sweeping point that extrapolates beyond Sabbath observance. He asserts His Lordship over an entire range of institutional practices. Of these, the Sabbath was probably the most revered and explosive. Jesus shows, in effect, that He is the new point of reunion with the Father. His unity with God is not simply a verbal assertion. He shows and assumes it by His manner of life. Jesus refers to the precedent of David to indicate that the past is not the preserve of traditionalists alone. The past is a creative reservoir for those who seek to move forward boldly and creatively. For the Lord to so openly question Sabbath observance was to place Himself above the Law. That is the precise point. For us, this means that the Lordship of Jesus is our link with the Father. Any type of excessive legalism evidences a lack of confidence in that Lordship. There is no other bridge remaining or needed between ourselves and the Father.

Point

Reconciliation with God is a real historical event as well as a real spiritual event in our lives. It is as real as we are.

MONDAY — Twenty-Third Week of the Year
Col 1:24-2:3   *Lk 6:6-11*

First Reading

The great message and mystery Paul has dedicated his life to announcing is the mystery of Christ alive in His disciples. This is a truth that is not often fully appreciated by Christians. Our Lord does not dwell in some remote heaven. The power and majesty of Christ exists within us. The risen and transformed Christ is now capable of existing within His followers, through His Spirit, as the secret energy that spurs our minds, emotions, wills and entire life. For this reason, Paul states that it is the energy of Christ that impels him to work so assiduously for the ministry. Jesus is the force, through His Spirit, who provides the drive of the Christian faith, hope and love in each of us. We are following not a distant, hidden Lord, but a Lord who lives and loves through us.

Gospel Reading

The healing of a man with a withered hand provides the occasion for Jesus to state that His mission is to give back life to those who have lost it. Throughout the entire set of healings which Jesus performs, He seeks to restore what is broken and to heal what is wounded. As we continue the Lord's ministry, we not only seek to imitate Him in the work He began but to allow the Lord Himself to continue His ministry through us. We are instruments in the great ongoing work of reconciliation. It is vital to recall that Christ Himself is the drive behind our Christian life.

Point

We are ministers and agents of the Risen Lord.

TUESDAY — Twenty-Third Week of the Year
Col 2:6-15   *Lk 6:12-19*

First Reading

The Christians at Colossae were locked into superstition and astrology. In this first reading, Paul makes his central point of the letter: All you need is Christ! In Christ, the fullness of God resides in bodily form. If God was completely in Christ, then the salvation offered us in Jesus is also complete. We need nothing further: no supplements, lucky charms, mantras or astrology charts. Christ took our bill and marked it "paid in full" and posted it for everyone to see on Calvary. Jesus took all of these subsidiary powers and led them away as a chain gang. Paul does not deny that these powers exist. He affirms Jesus to be more powerful than any of them individually or collectively. Today, many of us claim not to believe in ouija boards, palmistry or psychic phenomena. Many, however, are obsessed by the paranormal and preternatural. Even when we refer to these forces in humor, it is important that we remember that Jesus is more powerful than all of them.

Gospel Reading

This power of Christ has been transmitted to us through the Church. In this Gospel reading, after a night of communion with His Father, Jesus chooses the Twelve and the new Israel is born. Just as Jacob's blessing passed to his twelve sons, so Jesus' message and power will pass through His apostles as they transmit that power in various ways through teachers, deacons, priests and prophets. It is important that we recall that our use of images, medallions and blessings of various sorts all serve as reminders of the all-sufficient power of Jesus. They are not magical devices that operate apart from our faith. At their best, they remind us in times of sickness, temptation, self-doubt and loneliness of the love power of Jesus that comes to us through the community He founded.

Point

Sacred objects and blessings remind us of that river of life that flows in and through us from Jesus alone.

WEDNESDAY — Twenty-Third Week of the Year
Col 3:1-11   *Lk 6:20-26*

First Reading

Paul tells some of the semi-superstitious Christians at Colossae to set their hearts not on magical practices but on Christ in His glory. They are to build their lives on what lasts and not on what fades. They have been changed and have new Easter life in them. If we live in our old way with this new life within us, we create conflict, tension and dissonance. It is much like an individual who realizes fraud to be wrong but continues to deceive and shade the truth because everyone else does so. His or her experience is like that of being caught in a vise. Paul indicates that in such a situation, one of two things will happen. Either we will continue in our ways and strangle the eternal life begun in us or we will have to kill our old ways off and live like the new creation we are. Living as the new creation is difficult at first but it becomes easier as our inner and outer life come into harmony.

Gospel Reading

This Gospel reading makes the same point from a different angle. The Lord's pronouncement that the poor, hungry, sorrowful and hated are blessed sounds strange to us until we remember that Luke's Gospel was written for the poor, hungry, sorrowful and hated. Of course, Jesus is speaking here of general types. The poor are blessed because their illusions about life have been ripped away. They know their need. Typically, the rich and popular live on the surface of life. They have not confronted their personal limits. Like the celebrity who skyrockets to overnight fame without experiencing the underside of life that accompanies failure, the affluent often have not seen the awesome power of personal darkness.

Point

Both readings remind us that the deepest touchstone of reality is inward. Paul: let the outer life reflect the inner Spirit you have received. Jesus: We allow God to touch us in our deepest self when we know our need.

THURSDAY — Twenty-Third Week of the Year
Col 3:12-17   *Lk 6:27-38*

First Reading

Paul ends his letter to the Colossians with an exhortation to practice various virtues: kindness, humility, patience. The binding force that draws them all together and makes them coherent is love. All the virtues we often itemize and anatomize are applications of that fundamental posture of love. Love is not easily defined. We might define it by simply listing its characteristics which then yields a list of virtues. There is no way to express how the virtues function in an individual's life concretely. It is a function of Christian love. The more love we have in our heart toward God and others, the more easily all of these components of the Christian life fit together and express themselves in an effective way.

Gospel Reading

Jesus illustrates the serious and reaching demands of love. How He articulates the demands of Gospel living enables us to realize how narrow and confined our notion of Christian living can be. We settle into standard ways of doing things and certain traditional forms of compromising the Gospel. A reading such as this vividly recalls us to the really radical and thorough nature of the Gospel call. The Lord invites us not simply to react to evil but to take the offensive through forgiveness. He reminds us as well of the demanding and suffering component of love. When love today is so readily romanticized and trivialized, the Gospel reminds us that love is indeed sacrificial and other-directed. It is expressed not by warm feelings within but by what we pour out for others.

Point

There is no way of thoroughly defining the requirements of the Christian way of life. The attitude of love which we receive from the Holy Spirit becomes the source of our expression of faith.

FRIDAY — Twenty-Third Week of the Year
1 Tm 1:1-2,12-14   *Lk 6:39-42*

First Reading

The Church turning inward is the subject of this first letter to Timothy. When this letter was written, the Christian movement was becoming institutionalized. Questions were arising as to how to deal with deacons, bishops, widows and other women in the Church. No longer was Christianity a private, small ad lib movement from an organizational point of view. In this letter, we will witness the early Church becoming increasingly aware of its own structure and politics. The reading of this letter enables us to do some hard thinking about how we have assembled the charisms of a parish, how we use our gifts, how we settle our disputes, how we reach out to those who feel alienated from the Church.

Gospel Reading

The need for self-criticism provides the theme of today's Gospel reading. The blind cannot lead the blind. The Church does not exist in a bubble. When we pass the Church door we do not leave our biases and prejudices outside. There have been times in the Church's life when slavery was condoned and churches were segregated. These and many other such things occurred because the community of Jesus is more immersed in culture than we often care to admit. It is necessary, therefore, in the light of the New Testament, to examine our collective conscience. We cannot simply say that we have arrived and are renewed. "Now, let's freeze it and sell it!" Our own recent past reminds us that we are slowly continuing to grow into the image of Christ.

Point

The journey is the essence of the Church's life. We are not yet the Church triumphant.

SATURDAY — Twenty-Third Week of the Year
1 Tm 1:15-17   *Lk 6:43-49*

First Reading

We are all sinners. This old phrase carries within itself a great meaning that Paul exploits in today's first reading. We fall short of the glory of God, yet God has saved us. The fact that a parish with all of its shortcomings can still claim to be the Body of Christ shows that perfection is not a prerequisite for entry into the kingdom. Furthermore, our own failures both individually and institutionally should make us more compassionate toward others. Our denouncements of sin should be uncompromising and clear. Our relationships with those who have sinned, however, should be marked by compassion and love. This is exactly the model we see in Jesus. While His criticism of sin was always clear, His communion with sinners was so natural as to be a source of popular scandal. When we remember our own sins, however private, we will be more able to deal personally with those whose lives are not textbook perfect.

Gospel Reading

It is not our claims of discipleship but our practice of it that brings us salvation. We are called to put Jesus' words and deeds into practice. That implementation of Gospel living is the rock on which a life can be built. To keep the Gospel only at the level of theory, to be dislodged by another theory that later comes our way, is to build on sand. In such a case, the assurance and confidence promised us from Gospel living will always remain elusive. Those whose knowledge of the Gospel life is theoretical can become extremely judgmental and intolerant of the failures of others. It is only when we grow through the difficult work of trying to put the Lord's words into practice that we learn compassion. This enables us to appreciate our solidarity with all human beings in their search for God.

Point

The practice of the Christian life leads us to an experience of understanding and compassion. We come to realize the mind of Christ.

MONDAY — Twenty-Fourth Week of the Year
1 Tm 2:1-8   *Lk 7:1-10*

First Reading

The first letter to Timothy comes from a time when the fluid Christian movement was starting to settle down and become institutionalized. The early Christians were no longer waiting for the world to end but had to deal with and set up relationships in the society around them. In this reading, Paul recommends prayer not simply for fellow-Christians but for everyone, especially those in authority. After all, the Lord gave His life to ransom everybody whether they are Christian or not. Paul especially recommends prayer for the government because it helps to keep the peace. The Church does not exist in a hermetically sealed jar. Whether we choose to acknowledge it or not, by its very existence the Church is a political institution. All elements of life around us, religious and secular, influence our spiritual life and should enter our conversation with the Lord. Through prayer, we bring our world here.

Gospel Reading

This Roman officer evidently had good relationships with the Jews as well as with his own servant. In a prelude to the post-Pentecost Gentile mission, Jesus remarks on the officer's faith and answers his petition by healing the servant. It might be a thoroughly proper application of this scene to say that the Lord not only answers the prayers of Christians and Jews, but of Buddhists and Moslems as well. Two points emerge from this incident for our consideration. First, we continue Jesus' ministry to all people and not simply to fellow-Christians. Secondly, the Church is the center of a huge community of faith. People of tremendous good will surround us although they are not specifically Christian. We bring them into our liturgy in prayer if not yet in body.

Point

Through our life and prayers, the world we know is brought here, placed on the altar and inserted into the prayer of Jesus.

TUESDAY — Twenty-Fourth Week of the Year
1 Tm 3:1-13   *Lk 7:11-17*

First Reading

Paul lists the qualities necessary to be a good bishop and deacon. These qualifications reveal a great deal about the early Church. These bishops were Church administrators and not successors of the Apostles in the full sense as "original eyewitnesses." In that sense, the Twelve could have no successors. But in terms of handing on the tradition and maintaining harmony in the local church, these bishops succeeded to apostolic functions. Paul does not seek brilliance, soaring sanctity or fanatical zeal. The qualifications listed speak of a man of balance who can recognize charisms in others while being a father to all interests in the Church. Essentially, Paul is looking for balance and maturity. The same is true for deacons who function as administrators — the equivalent of our finance and parish councils. They are to be people of moderation as well. These same qualities, with slight modification, apply to Church officials today. Zeal for the Gospel does not require that we read out of the Church those who differ with us on questions of method, emphasis and style.

Gospel Reading

Bringing the dead to life is as dramatic an event in our day as it was in the time of Jesus. There are many kinds of death. There is physical death as well as the spiritual death of sin, the ecclesial death of ostracism, the canonical death of suspension, the intellectual death of silenced thinkers, the emotional death of creative exuberance suppressed. As ministers of the Lord, we are called to summon all of these people to new life. The Church should be a place not where people come to die but where they can come to receive new vigor and life.

Point

The business of a parish is not death but birth.

WEDNESDAY — Twenty-Fourth Week of the Year
1 Tm 3:14-16   *Lk 7:31-35*

First Reading

The Church's role as the pillar and bulwark of truth, to which Paul alludes in today's first reading, exposes another dimension of our ecclesial existence. The Church is more than a community of people. It also stands for something. The Church is not an apologist for economic systems, political arrangements or cultural taboos. The Church stands, as Paul tells us, for Jesus Christ — incarnate, risen and now made glorious. That core event of our preaching has implications for economic and social policy to which the Church cannot be blind. But the Church's truth is essentially evangelical. That Gospel truth will be differently applied in various places. The great danger is to take applied truth and to treat it as evangelical. Our commitment to the Risen Lord might cause us to criticize certain economic dislocations in our society in a public way. But that critique is not a normative and universal part of the Gospel message. We are committed to the Lord and not to ideology.

Gospel Reading

It is no surprise, therefore, that the Church's application of the Gospel message will differ around the world. The values for which the Church stands in a socialist society will be applied differently in a capitalist one. The values remain the same, the application differs. The result is often a thoroughgoing unpopularity. This was the response the Lord met. When the Baptist spoke of repentance, he was considered too fanatical. When Jesus spoke of repentance, He was considered too lax. The values were the same, the context differed. The refusal to follow either was justified by any available excuse. The charge of inconsistency against the Church as being too otherworldly or too involved in this world derives not from the search for ideological purity or theoretical consistency. It comes very often from a refusal to serve the Lord.

Point

Although the Church's message is applied differently in various social situations and the refusal to listen is justified differently in various contexts — the basic dynamism remains the same. People refuse the light.

THURSDAY — Twenty-Fourth Week of the Year
1 Tm 4:12-16   *Lk 7:36-50*

First Reading

Timothy was evidently very young. Paul reminds him of the office and spirit he has received. As representative of the Church, he speaks the Gospel with derived authority. That authority flows in large part from ordination. In addition to the credibility that attaches to ascribed status, there is a credibility he must earn. Paul therefore urges him to be an example of love, faith and purity. His life style should be exemplary, his learning helpful to others and his prayer constant. Official positions in the Church carry with them a great deal of authority. Those who occupy these positions must become worthy of them by fulfilling the expectations inherent in those offices. Those who preach must study and meditate on the Word. Those who administer must not only know the Word but become adept at administrative technique. It is a great temptation to let the status we are given in the Church canonize us so that we feel no need of further study or development — which in fact we do owe to that office and to the Church. The aura of holiness that comes, for example, with the office of priest/ presbyter does not excuse its holder from the personal search for deeper prayer and knowledge of Jesus.

Gospel Reading

Public ascriptions of status can be deceptive. The woman was known to be a sinner, but she had a heart filled with repentant love. The Pharisee represented a law that allowed for forgiveness. Yet, he was only able to notice sin and not to discover in that woman's gesture a search for God. He questioned how much of a prophet Jesus could be to allow this woman to so approach Him. Jesus showed Himself to be a magnificent prophet in His ability to look into both the Pharisee's heart and that of the woman and see which was filled with love. The Lord warns the Pharisees and us not to be too hasty in our attribution of holiness or sin to the outward behavior of others. We are unable to read the heart. Priests sin and sinners pray. We must leave final judgment to God.

Point

Outward appearances can be controlled and deceptive. We should try to become in fact what we try to appear to be to others.

FRIDAY — Twenty-Fourth Week of the Year
1 Tm 6:2-12   *Lk 8:1-3*

First Reading

Religion can be a source of great gain, says Paul to Timothy. He tells him to teach sound doctrine and not a version of religion that people like to hear — a version which fails to challenge. Gain from religion can take many forms. There are those who would profit financially from religion. Today's reading specifically refers to them. But people can also profit politically, vocationally, or socially by using religion as a tool of social control. There are many ways of using the institutions of religion for purposes that are essentially crass and self-centered. Such unfortunate misuse of religion does not completely vitiate the Church's essential mission. The human search for healing as well as God's outreach to mankind can be commercialized, trivialized, packaged, advertised — but they cannot be killed. The reality of God's Word is stronger than human attempts to manipulate it for secular purposes. The Word of God lives through God's Spirit which cannot be chained or tamed.

Gospel Reading

We have a brief look at some of the people who followed Jesus. Women are extremely important figures in Luke's Gospel. They were among the people who were attracted to His preaching and who had, in some way, been touched by it. People followed the Lord for all kinds of reasons. The Lord was always able to take that search for wholeness and discover within it some avenue to release faith within a person. Even with those people who are attracted to the Church for less than pure motives, the Lord can in some unexpected way touch them and find in their hearts a place of faith from which greater faith can be built. We must be careful not to dismiss those who have used the Church. Some tiny island of faith may remain in them from which they can be renewed.

Point

The effort to manipulate religion is as old as is the effort to find God. God survives our human efforts to use Him.

SATURDAY — Twenty-Fourth Week of the Year
1 Tm 6:13-16   *Lk 8:4-15*

First Reading

The preaching of the Word has always met with mixed success. Paul tells Timothy that after he does his best to speak God's Word, he should rest secure in the fact that he has done his job. There is no automatic guarantee of immediate success. As Christians, if we live our lives as best we can, we stand without reproach before the Lord. Whether others will accept the Word and example we have given is a matter for which they themselves will have to answer before the Lord. We cannot entrap people into the Church. Human response is, by legal and canonical definition, freely given. As agents of the Lord, we simply place ourselves at His disposal. That is our mission for which the Lord will give us an eternal reward.

Gospel Reading

The parable of the seed that was sown onto all kinds of ground was a great comfort to the early Church. We all live, at times, with an unshared vision. We see things and futures that others are unable or refuse to see. It puzzles us as to why they can be so blind. Thus it was for the early Church. The Gospel of life and love which they lived and experienced did not receive universal acceptance. Some became Christians and then dropped away. Others left during persecution. All of this puzzled the early Church. For them, Luke recounts the Lord's parable of the seed. Its message coincides with that of the first reading. All we can do is our best to sow the seed widely. Where it lands and how it grows depends upon the ground. Through this parable, the Christians were assured that failure to find unanimous acceptance of the Word was not necessarily their fault but the result of factors beyond their immediate control. Even the failures of the early Church fell within God's design.

Point

We can control the sowing of the seed. We cannot control the growth that takes place in that mysterious chemistry between soil and seed.

MONDAY — Twenty-Fifth Week of the Year
Ezr 1:1-6   *Lk 8:16-18*

First Reading

As we return to the Old Testament story, we might reorient ourselves. We have seen the story of Abraham, Moses, Joshua, the Judges, the Kings, the divided kingdom, the deportation of the northern kingdom (Israel) by Assyria and the southern kingdom (Judah) by Babylon. Eventually, the Persians defeated Babylon. This is the point at which we re-enter the story. Cyrus, the Persian king, allowed the exiled people of Judah to return to their homeland. They have become a changed people in this interval. Their political illusions are gone. From this point, they will be called Jews (Judah-ites). During the exile, they zeroed in on their religious identity: Temple, priesthood and Law. The exile saw the birth of a new class of students of the Torah Law called Scribes , who combined an expertise in the analysis of the Law together with an anti-Gentile paranoia. It was, after all, the mingling with Gentiles that took them into exile in the first place. In retrospect, the exile provided a necessary purgation much as the loss of the Papal States was actually a liberation for the Church. The exile was not simply a set of negatives. It eliminated a great deal of accumulated junk in the national soul and allowed the people to focus on their spiritual identity.

Gospel Reading

The Lord speaks about the light on a stand which is to be kept burning brightly. What is that light? This image follows the parable of the sower. The light might be the Word of God, the Holy Spirit, or the disciples themselves. The image suggests that the light is not to be hidden but to be distributed and made public and conspicuous. The many things that occur in our lives have the potential to bring clarity into our spiritual life. Some people do not allow that to happen. They disconnect everyday life from their spiritual life. The result is that they expect the Lord to speak only in visions. In fact, the Lord does not speak exclusively or primarily in private revelations. The Lord speaks to us through events as He calls us into a brighter, clearer and purer experience of the light.

Point

Events, good and bad, bring clarity to our light.

TUESDAY — Twenty-Fifth Week of the Year
Ezr 6:7-8, 12, 14-20   *Lk 8:19-21*

First Reading

Building the Temple was not as easy as today's first reading might imply. The elite of the people had originally been sent into exile. Throughout those years, the locals who had remained behind developed their own folk religion, their own ranking of priests and their own cadre of corrupt officials. It was no easy task, therefore, to rebuild the Temple. Finally, after a great deal of grief from the locals as well as the enemies of the returnees, it was built. These tensions indicated not only how difficult it was to build the Temple but how hard it was to rebuild the community. There are similar tensions in most parishes between newcomers and the founding families. Building the community is more critical than constructing a building, because the community shares and carries the tradition. The enduring achievement of Ezra and Nehemiah was their creation of a cohesive community (more or less), around Jerusalem after the exile. We all belong to several communities: political, social, professional and recreational. The most vital community to which we belong is our family, which ought to be mainly a community of faith.

Gospel Reading

The Lord speaks about the deep ties that link His disciples to Him and to each other. In the Church, we are bonded to people around the world, to fellow Christians of the past and of the future. We belong to Jesus through call and discipleship. This was the same with Mary and Jesus' own extended family. The ties of faith, though, are more critical even than those of blood. We honor Mary less for her genetic connection to Jesus than for her faith and love. Faith binds a diverse group of people together. We are composed of the powerful and the powerless. We are a community that is one, holy, catholic and apostolic. Mass in a parish church rescues us from romantic fantasies about the universal Church and reminds us that we are a Church of very human beings who are answering the Lord's call to each of us.

Point

Within the diverse collection of people we call the Church, Jesus is mysteriously present as Lord.

WEDNESDAY — Twenty-Fifth Week of the Year
Ezr 9:5-9   *Lk 9:1-6*

First Reading

Ezra offers a prayer of thanksgiving to God after the Temple had been rebuilt. He recounts the history of Israel, their repeated failures and the just judgment God pronounced upon them in sending them into exile. Here, he expresses gratitude for the fact that God did not abandon them but allowed them to return and begin again. This is a prayer that could only be uttered after the exile. The national period of penance was over and, in the person of Ezra, the people realize the great grace given them. This prayer is a theological interpretation of the exile of Judah and perhaps of every individual's personal experience of exile. After we have sinned and realize the enormity of what we have done, we can appreciate the tremendous grace which the opportunity to begin again always is.

Gospel Reading

In these missionary instructions, the Lord sends the Twelve to receive some "hands on" experience in preaching the Word and continuing the ministry. The instructions are geared toward achieving the widest possible dissemination of word and ministry. The simplicity of life style that Jesus requires is a combination of strategy, custom and trust in God. It is a great grace to us that missionaries were sent to the homes of our ancestors to preach the Gospel. Were it not for those poor and frequently martyred messengers of the Gospel, armed only with the Lord's Word, the wealthy and prosperous parishes we find in our country would not exist. This expansionist thrust of the Church to reach out is not only geographical. It also requires us to thrust deeper into the faith we have received and to intensify our experience as the community of the Lord. Our own realization of the gift of faith should enable us to contribute toward those missionaries who now carry the faith elsewhere.

Point

The more we appreciate the giftedness of our faith, the more we are eager to share it with others.

THURSDAY — Twenty-Fifth Week of the Year
Hg 1:1-8   *Lk 9:7-9*

First Reading

Haggai is a prophet among the returned exiles. There was no frantic rush to return to a broken homeland among the exiles. Once they had returned, enthusiasm was dampened to say the least. This highlights the leadership of Ezra and the prophets such as Haggai. Eighteen years after the new foundations of the Temple were laid, it remained unbuilt. Haggai rides herd on the people in today's first reading to complete the work. The Book of Ezra had attributed the blame to enemies of the returnees. Haggai blames the returned exiles for being lazy. Within a four month period he begged, cajoled, warned and berated the people into finishing the Temple project. During the exile, the Judah-ites focused increasingly on Law, Temple, and ritual more in metaphor than in fact. Haggai forces them to face the brute fact that the Temple and its focal place in Jewish life must be more than a dream. We can contrast Haggai with Amos. Amos excoriated ritual and emphasized social concern. Now, social concern is placed on the back burner and concern shifts toward Temple and ritual.

Gospel Reading

The emphasis on things of the Temple continued into the Lord's time. Jesus tries to restore balance by retrieving the pre-exilic tradition. This made Him puzzling to people, as we can see in today's Gospel reading. They thought Him to be Elijah or one of the old-time prophets come back to life. The tension between liturgy and social justice is a healthy one. In a liturgy that is properly celebrated, divisions along the lines of age, sex, race and wealth are slowly overcome. We learn respect for others and for the creation "which earth has given and human hands have made." We overcome our natural inclination toward self-interest and place ourselves in a universe of wider concern. It enables us to see our successes and failures as part of a larger family. This can give us energy, light and comfort.

Point

Liturgy and life should connect and not separate.

FRIDAY — Twenty-Fifth Week of the Year
Hg 1:15-2:9   *Lk 9:18-22*

First Reading

Haggai continues to deliver oracles about the rebuilt Temple. Evidently, it did not measure up to the memory of the former Temple. Haggai speaks about the brick and mortar edifice. There is in Scripture study a construct called the "sensus plenior," the fuller sense. This is a meaning God intended which goes beyond the literal meaning of words meant by a prophet. Prophetic references to the "new Jerusalem," for example, literally referred to the revived city. The deeper spiritual sense, however, is the spiritual community and kingdom of God. Although Haggai speaks about the building, the fuller sense refers to Jesus Christ. In the Lord Jesus and not in any collection of mortar and stone do we have the fulfillment of every one of God's Old Testament promises of glory and majesty. Jesus is the new Temple and place of God's presence to us.

Gospel Reading

This makes today's Gospel reading more poignant. Jesus is about to begin His journey to Jerusalem. On the way, He stops and asks whether anybody has understood anything He has said and done thus far. "Who do they say I am?" Peter responds that Jesus is the Messiah, the fulfillment of Old Testament hopes. He had been picking up all the small signals Jesus had been sending out. Jesus knew, as well, about those dreams of Messianic glory and kingship that were sizzling in the disciples' minds. For that reason, He began to tell them that He must suffer and die and only then be raised up. Jesus explained to them and to Peter the fuller meaning of Peter's own words. The Messiah would have spiritual, not political glory.

Point

In order for the kingdom to become public, we must first experience its glory within our lives.

SATURDAY — Twenty-Fifth Week of the Year
Zc 2:5-9, 14-15   *Lk 9:43-45*

First Reading

Deeper meanings pervade both of today's readings. Zechariah was a contemporary of Haggai during the time after the exile. He speaks about the restored Temple and the rebuilt Jerusalem. His vision portrays a man seeking to measure out the geographical dimensions of the city. An angel responds that this city is on a different level than geography. It is useless to plan because the future is so great that millions of people will be drawn here. This city crosses space and time. It is the very abode of God which He has encircled with fire. The great Jerusalem is the place where God dwells: human hearts and souls. It cannot be confined or measured. It is a city that encompasses every nation and age. It is wider than the Church and smaller than the Church. There are no political or religious boundaries that exactly coincide with it. Its population is composed of those whose hearts are opened to the Lord. He alone knows their number.

Gospel Reading

Jesus' prediction of suffering did not fall on deaf as much as on uncomprehending ears. What it meant for the Messiah to suffer contradicted everything they had ever been told or taught to expect. Perhaps, in some incipient way, the disciples realized they were in the presence of mystery. They did not pursue the point with the Lord. Later, the meaning of His words would become very clear. They would see His exact meaning played out before their eyes. Only after the Resurrection would it all click as they recalled these words and their own amazing incomprehension. So much happens in the Church and in our own lives that we cannot fully understand. We know that we are in the middle of great events. All we can do is to have faith that the Lord's promises to us will be fulfilled. In the end, the rationale of all suffering, pain and joy will be made clear.

Point

Like the new Jerusalem, the plan of God does not submit itself to our precise comprehension and measurement. We are in the presence of mystery that only the Lord will unlock for us in His own time.

MONDAY — Twenty-Sixth Week of the Year
Zc 8:1-8   Lk 9:46-50

First Reading

Zechariah lived about the same time as Haggai and joined with him in predicting the dawn of a new era once the Temple was rebuilt. Zechariah had a particular historical contemporary in mind as the promised Messiah. The first part of his book contains a series of visions of what the reign of this Messiah will imply. These visions have a far more inspired reference and import than an historical figure named Zerubbabel. We can have a better understanding of today's first reading if we recall that during the exile, Jerusalem had become something very akin to a ghost town. It was a city almost completely ruined both in building and in spirit. In this part of his prophecy, Zechariah looks forward to a city come back to life with young and old teeming in its streets. He sees a community reborn. The deeper meaning of his words, not realized by Zechariah himself, lay in the city of God. He points to a city of human beings who would be God's people in the world. God would bring new life to His people who have become a remnant. They will thrive in the Spirit.

Gospel Reading

The Lord briefly describes those who compose the people of God by saying that whoever welcomes a child welcomes Him. Children were the least important members of society. Jesus indicates that whoever is prepared to spend his or her life in serving and helping people who do not matter much in the eyes of the world is serving Him and the Father (consciously or not). They are all people of God. The category "people of God" places emphasis less on superficial similarities or differences than on the real points of unity among the people on earth. It points to a community of faith that appears fragmented along denominational lines but is really deeply united in the Spirit.

Point

The most authentic urge deep within people is not toward division but toward unity.

TUESDAY — Twenty-Sixth Week of the Year
Zc 8:20-23   Lk 9:51-56

First Reading

Zechariah again looks forward to a time when all the people of God would gather in Jerusalem to seek the Lord together. We should recall that after the exile, Jewish consciousness — at its best moments — came to see universal restoration and the unity of the human family as the real goal of the Covenant, Torah and Temple. Before the exile, an ardent exclusivism prevailed in the religious consciousness of the people of Judah. Now, after their national torment, the best postexilic prophetic visions saw Judah as entrusted with a mission deeper than Torah preservation. They were to invite all people to Jerusalem. As time went on, that great postexilic vision became debased. But this great vision has been inherited by the Church. The Acts of the Apostles recalls a period of narrow exclusivism followed by persecution and the opening of the Gentile mission to the ends of the earth.

Gospel Reading

In a section distinctive to Luke's Gospel, Jesus begins His journey to Jerusalem and the consummation of His earthly ministry. The rest of Luke's Gospel will be taken up with the historical details and theological implications of that mission. In today's reading, some of Jesus' disciples precede Him through a Samaritan town. The Samaritans, traditionally hostile to the Jews, would not welcome Jesus because He was going to Jerusalem. The Apostles are anxious for immediate judgment. Jesus refuses to do so and continues the journey. He refuses to sanction old feuds. This foreshadows the possibility of repentance for all people. In the Acts of the Apostles, after the Jerusalem Jews persecute and scatter the early Church, the first people to receive the apostolic preaching with enthusiasm are the Samaritans. What was hidden from them at this point became plain after Pentecost through the preaching of the deacon Philip. Thus the possibility of a national conversion is always available.

Point

An initial refusal can often become the start of a long conversion process.

WEDNESDAY — Twenty-Sixth Week of the Year
Ne 2:1-8   *Lk 9:57-62*

First Reading

To this point, we have read about Ezra and the religious side of the return from exile with the rebuilding of the Temple. Ezra was the religious leader. Nehemiah was the political leader. When Nehemiah heard in Persia of the condition of Jerusalem, with its people in distress, the walls down and the city gutted, he wept. He was then sent by the king to rebuild the city. He came to Jerusalem, surveyed the broken walls and moved priests and people to start rebuilding. The Book of Nehemiah lists the various gates entering the city: Fishgate, Valleygate, Dunggate, Springgate, Sheepgate and Watergate. It even includes lists of the unions that helped rebuild the walls. The rebuilding was no easy task. Nehemiah realized that the community could not be revived without it.

Gospel Reading

Jesus calls for full-time discipleship. It requires that we love the Lord more than we do our property (the Son of Man has no home) and that we follow Him without delay (not to wait for parents to die). The intensity of our discipleship is measured as well by the extent to which we let our faith seep out into the world of politics, work and human relations. The depth of our commitment to Jesus is evidenced by whether we let our discipleship show in the way we vote, spend, recreate and deal with others. To leave all behind and follow the Lord in a cloistered or monastic setting is one form of discipleship. It is just as demanding to remain in the world as a light and a beacon.

Point

The life of the Holy Spirit in us is not a closed circuit. We are called to be mature channels for the entry of God's love and spirit into our world.

THURSDAY — Twenty-Sixth Week of the Year
Ne 8:1-4, 5-6, 7-12   *Lk 10:1-12*

First Reading

Rebuilding the walls of the city was an easier task for Nehemiah than was rebuilding the community inside the walls. Within, the wealthy were bilking the poor and taking their sons and daughters in hock. Nehemiah immediately forbade usury. Finally, after the walls were reconstructed, the time came to rebuild the community. Ezra the scribe read the Law at the Watergate and there the people renewed the covenant. This restoration of Jerusalem remained until Herod extensively remodeled both city and Temple. Ezra and Nehemiah essentially created a theocracy. The people were expected to follow the Law totally, as every aspect of life was closely regulated. This became a characteristic of Judaism into Jesus' time. The exile had shifted focus to the Law as the only glue that could hold a broken people together. Preoccupation with obedience to the Torah Law became excessive. This was the Judaism Jesus confronted.

Gospel Reading

Trying to revive the ancient consciousness of promise and covenant by breaking the hold of excessive legalism was not easy. Jesus knew that His own lifetime would not be enough to make people aware that the Law was not God, that the obedience God required was far deeper than anything that could be captured in the Law. For this reason, Jesus created a community to continue His message. In today's Gospel reading, He sends a further seventy-two to go throughout the villages to announce the good news that the hold of sin was broken and that the kingdom of God was at hand. The import and urgency of that message required that it be spread broadly and faithfully. Jesus would break the hold of evil and, after Easter, would empower His community to survive with this message until the end of time.

Point

Slavery to Law in place of freedom in God's Spirit brings its own kind of judgment.

FRIDAY — Twenty-Sixth Week of the Year
Bar 1:15-22   *Lk 10:13-16*

First Reading

The Book of the prophet Baruch is allegedly by the secretary of Jeremiah. Scholars generally agree, however, that it was written after the exile. In fact, some date it after the birth of

Christ. The readings we have today and tomorrow are a liturgical confession of sin. We see in today's reading a distillation of the post-exilic realization of what went wrong in the decades before the exile. The reading captures the religious consciousness of a people after their return to the promised land. It acknowledges that the Lord's ways are just. The exile was no accident or curse. It was the inevitable consequence of the broken covenant and idolatry of the years preceding it. The words of the prophets had been disregarded, and the Torah Law was broken. Buried deep inside this admission is the resolution that the priests and leaders of the people would ensure that the Law was never broken again. The Law would now be enforced with a vengeance.

Gospel Reading

The woe the Lord pronounces follows the commissioning of the seventy-two to preach the Word. This captures in miniature what would happen in the Church's mission after the Ascension. The Jewish towns of Chorazin and Bethsaida will reject the apostolic preaching. These towns really stand for the Jews who had so tightly constricted their minds and hearts with legal observance that they were not open to the liberating Word of the Lord. Jesus concludes that whoever listens to His disciples, hears Him. This presaged the Jewish rejection of the Christian preaching and the remarkable and unexpected openness of Samaritans and Gentiles to the Gospel message. Jesus points out that there is no difference between those who hear the teaching of the Church and those who were present on the paths of Galilee as He walked and talked. Both are given the Word of life.

Point

Law is an important guide. But it is not the liberating Word of life.

SATURDAY — Twenty-Sixth Week of the Year
Bar 4:5-12,27-29   *Lk 10:17-24*

First Reading

Baruch writes in tones that remind us of Isaiah of Babylon's message of hope from the end of the exile. In a power filled poetic image, Jerusalem is personified as representing the spirit of obedience and covenant toward which her people were always to have aspired. She speaks, almost in God's name, of the regret and mourning that the exile brought upon her and her children. As Jerusalem is wounded by the punishment of her children, it reminds us that God is not a passive spectator to our sin. His love for each of us is real. Our sin against Him is real. When we sin we do much more than violate a transcendent law. To state it directly, we hurt God. We refuse His offer of love and break the covenant bond between us. Sin is more than a legal violation. It is a personal injury of God. It is part of the great drama of salvation that we mortal beings have it in our power to affect the immense God of the universe. These words may sound like pulpit rhetoric until we see Calvary.

Gospel Reading

The disciples return enthused that demons were subject to them when they preached in the Lord's name. After their wonder at the power of the Gospel, Jesus reminds them that He is more powerful than Satan. Yet, more grand than the empirical effects of the Gospel is the effort of every Christian to try to live and preach the Gospel with sincerity. Jesus utters a prayer of thanks to the Father and tells His disciples that this power they have to liberate individuals is the greatest power on earth. It is what the prophets had dreamed about. By this power, they can set an individual free to become the son or daughter of God that he or she was destined to be at birth. They are doing nothing less than restoring the original order of creation.

Point

Sin has real power to destroy. Grace has real power to heal and make whole.

MONDAY — Twenty-Seventh Week of the Year
Jon 1:1-2:1, 11   *Lk 10:25-37*

First Reading

The Book of Jonah comes from a period after the time of Ezra and Nehemiah. After the exile, a tremendous effort was mounted by the Jewish leaders and people to protect and preserve their distinctively Jewish identity. The focus was placed on Torah Law, Temple and priesthood. They constructed all kinds of spiritual and psychological walls against outsiders. The Book of Jonah is a reaction to that ethnocentrism. It makes a case for an ecumenism of sorts. The Book of Jonah views the forces which Ezra and Nehemiah had set in motion as having gone too far. In the story, Jonah is sent to preach to the Ninevites, Israel's ancient enemies. Jonah refuses the commission to these Assyrians. God's word was not for them. By a series of highly dramatic and strange events, Jonah is finally cast up on the shore of the place where the Lord wants him to go. In effect, God reminds Jonah and us that the message of salvation and forgiveness is for everyone. We should not restrict or confine God's love or our compassion.

Gospel Reading

Jesus stands in the ecumenical tradition of the Book of Jonah as we can see from today's parable. The priest and Levite hurried to the Temple with an alacrity and singlemindedness that would have made Ezra and Nehemiah proud. The one who stopped to help another human being was (gag — cough — gasp) a Samaritan. The lawyer had asked Jesus for a definition of neighbor, for the outlines of a class. Jesus responds by describing what it means to be a neighbor to another. Instead of dividing the world into neighbors and non-neighbors we should make sure that we always act as neighbor to others as best we can. It is a relationship rather than a category. The secular concern of the Samaritan was also a sign of the presence of God's kingdom.

Point

Ezra and Nehemiah were examples of passionate devotion to the God of Israel. Jesus reminds us that we should love our neighbor with the same passionate intensity.

TUESDAY — Twenty-Seventh Week of the Year
Jon 3:1-10   *Lk 10:38-42*

First Reading

The message finally got through to Jonah that he was to preach repentance to the pagan Assyrians. He marches back and forth through Nineveh proclaiming the word. His enthusiasm may well have been half-hearted in that he did not expect any response. To his astonishment, everyone repented from the king down. The evil of which Jonah thought he was to be the harbinger did not take place. The entire population of Nineveh was saved. We often carry stereotypes into our ministry and conversation with others. There are certain expected responses which we anticipate people will make. Very often, however, we are thrown off balance by the sudden surprise of their breaking out of our categories. In the end, people are individuals and each person must be encountered as an individual. The Lord came to save each person and not broad, amorphous classes of people.

Gospel Reading

Two sisters respond differently but authentically to the Lord. Martha is at work while Mary listens to the Word. Both are ways of obeying the Lord. Jesus endorses Mary's effort to hear the Word of life — an unusual privilege in those days when women were not allowed to receive rabbinic instruction. We all need to take the time to regroup and reposition ourselves in the presence of the Lord. We can become so caught up in the frantic fever of work and obligations that we do not take the time to look at the individual contours of all the relationships in which we are involved. We all develop a spiritual and social shorthand by which we standardize our responses to events. Such an approach is much easier in a busy world than seeking out the uniqueness of individuals that come our way. Mary reminds us that we should stop and make time to examine the special features of our family, social and professional lives. Each situation carries its own individual potential for grace and life.

Point

Situations of sin and grace are individual and not typical.

WEDNESDAY — Twenty-Seventh Week of the Year
Jon 4:1-11   *Lk 11:1-4*

First Reading

Nineveh repented and the prophet Jonah is disappointed. His mission as a prophet seemed to be robbed of all meaning.

There was no blazing wrath or fiery vengeance. He had no opportunity to say, "I told you so." This threw Jonah into the paradigmatic blue funk. He went outside the city to wait for its destruction on the outside chance that these pagans were really "faking it." While he was there, a plant grew up overnight and was destroyed by the morning sun the next day. Jonah complained to the Lord about the plant's needless destruction even though he had thirsted for Nineveh's total annihilation. Ocassionally we hear of people who are ready to "nuke" our national enemies while showing great compassion for the suffering of pet animals. The Jonah story ends with a reflection on the meaning of mercy. All the people of Nineveh, from the greatest to the least, were objects of God's love. This is the message of the Book of Jonah. The Jews did not have an exclusive distributorship for God's love and mercy.

Gospel Reading

We can carry the Jonah message to today's Gospel reading. The disciples ask Jesus to teach them to pray. More accurately, they want to know how to "ask" things of God. The Lord teaches them through the prayer that we have come to know as the "Our Father." Two main elements are distinctive to Jesus' approach to the Father. First is the acknowledgment of and submission to God's sovereignty and providence. The second places our individual and particular needs within that great design. So often, we reverse that order and come to see the providence of God as a tool of our special needs. This was actually what Jonah tried to do in turning God into an endorser of his own prejudices and biases.

Point

The things in our life that we cannot control we submit to the providence of God in whom we should have faith and confidence.

THURSDAY — Twenty-Seventh Week of the Year
Ml 3:13-20   *Lk 11:5-13*

First Reading

Malachi was a prophet after the exile when the second Temple was completed but before the city was rebuilt. In this interim period, enthusiasm waned. This book describes what was taking place in those years. The priests were offering junk food on the altar; there was a great deal of intermarriage ("I hate divorce, says the Lord"). To a dispirited people, Malachi states the Lord's message that "Lo, I am sending my messenger." Historically, this is interpreted to be Nehemiah who came with a program of thoroughgoing social reformation. The inspired reference is to John the Baptist. In today's first reading, the people ask what return they are receiving for their religious obedience. Malachi responds with the image of the record book. An account is being kept as a day approaches when the proud will become stubble. Malachi makes the effort to stretch the people's vision beyond this world. The configurations of power and success that we see do not reflect accurately the spiritual state of affairs.

Gospel Reading

The subject of prayer, how to "ask" God, continues. The Lord speaks of persistence and uses two images. The point of these images is not similarity but contrast. We are not wringing gifts from an unwilling God as though He throws us a bone to keep us quiet. Rather, Jesus indicates that if these people who do not want to respond are forced to answer the pleas they hear, how much more will our Father who knows our real needs respond to our prayers. God supplies our spiritual needs. Our prayers are usually framed in terms of material needs. Whatever else it might entail, God's answer is always in terms of our spiritual well-being which may not always be obvious to us.

Point

There is a larger scope to what we are and what we will be than is evident to us here and now.

FRIDAY — Twenty-Seventh Week of the Year
Jl 1:13-15; 2:1-2   *Lk 11:15-26*

First Reading

This first reading from the prophet Joel is a call to repent. The period is post-exilic. The priests are firmly in control of the restored Temple some fifty years after the prophet Malachi. The occasion for Joel's words is a locust plague which he saw as a symbol of a coming clash of good and evil. Increasingly, in this period after the exile, the spiritual writers will become preoccupied with the cosmic shape of the spiritual conflicts which until now had been experienced in local politics or individual souls. The exile seems to have switched their lenses to a higher power and they began to see a vast, mounting world-wide crisis that would bring the age to an end. Joel, in particular, speaks of the strength that must be mustered for the final battle. The strength required will not be political or military but spiritual.

Gospel Reading

The cosmic dimension of that ultimate battle took local form in the ministry of Jesus. The Lord speaks about a man who cleansed his house so that it was spotless. The purity was external. The demon returned and brought his friends because there was no spiritual strength, no inner resilience. Jesus' exor-

cisms were signs that the kingdom of God was irrupting into a
world that had not seen it come so directly and personally
before. The result was confrontation. It was not only a confrontation between Jesus and demons but between Jesus and de-
bilitated religion as well. In Him, the great clash which Malachi
predicted was taking place once and for all. The power and
strength of the Church is not political or financial. Its abiding
strength is spiritual. This is the one source of its strength that
Jesus promised would never be destroyed.

Point

*No one can take the Holy Spirit away from us. We are the
only ones who can cut off His influence.*

SATURDAY — Twenty-Seventh Week of the Year
Jl 4:12-21   *Lk 11:27-28*

First Reading

After the exile, there was a rise in an odd kind of writing
called apocalyptic prophecy which describes a vivid clash of
good and evil. Before the exile, prophets such as Isaiah, Amos
and Jeremiah criticized the nation for its sins. They predicted
destruction if no change took place. After the exile, the
prophets came to see that the greed, evil and imbalance among
people reflected far deeper forces at work in the universe. The
world was really a theater for the conflict between the forces of
good and evil. Such a conflict is systemic; its pressure is mounting until the final explosion in the valley of Jehoshaphat. What
was required was more than personal repentance which might
save individuals. The conflict will be eliminated by complete
transformation — a new heaven and a new earth. In today's first
reading, Joel describes the coming conflict. The grapes of wrath
are about to be trampled into a bloody wine. He sees the

conflict as between Gentiles (black hats) and Judah (white hats). We can see deeper meaning in his prophecy. We know that the conflict is essentially not between good and bad nations. No nation is spotless. Rather, the conflict is between the people of God and the people dedicated to evil and selfishness which transcends national boundaries.

Gospel Reading

In today's Gospel reading, Jesus indicates that this spiritual community called the Church is not defined by family ties, nationality or by listening to the Word of God. It is composed of those who hear the Word of God and seek to implement it. We Christians can read the prophet Joel in the light of Easter. The conflicts we experience are the tail end of the final conflict that has already taken place on Calvary. The final victory was achieved on Easter Sunday. The conflict we experience, like the light from stars long extinct, is the residue of that original conflict. It is real conflict but the outcome has long been decided. We can now draw strength and power from Jesus' victory. We experience that original battle not in its cosmic form but in a local way in our daily struggle of faith and love.

Point

The war is over. Our realization of that truth helps us in the battles we have yet to fight.

MONDAY — Twenty-Eighth Week of the Year
Rm 1:1-7   *Lk 11:29-32*

First Reading

We begin Paul's letter to the Romans, the longest and most dazzling, magnificent and influential letter he ever wrote. Every unconventional thinker in the Church has had recourse to it in one way or another. The setting of the letter is important. Paul's work in the Eastern Mediterranean was finished. He had established his seed churches and was preparing to go to Spain with a stopover in Rome. The Roman Church was not a community he had founded. This is the reason for the formal introduction in today's first reading. In this letter, he gathers some conclusions from his missionary experience among the Gentiles. Salvation, that is, God's life, is offered to all people through Jesus not because any individual deserves it but as a free gift from God. He describes the news of Jesus and His preaching of salvation as part of an ancient divine plan whose unfolding we can see throughout the Old Testament. God's purpose for mankind today is the same as it was in the beginning. There is no divine broken field-running. What seems to be erratic is really our groping understanding of that divine design. The same is true of our own life. God's purpose for us today is the same as when we were born. He continues to bring that purpose to fruition throughout all the fits and starts of our lives.

Gospel Reading

Jesus speaks about the sign of Jonah at which the Ninevites repented. That sign is the image of one man trying to awaken people without miracles to the spiritual facts of life. The Word of God is given to all people in many ways. Some receive it more clearly than others. All receive it as the silent movement of their conscience. The Word comes in some way to all people. We are accountable to the Lord for our response to that Word.

Point

God is not silent in any individual's life. Very often, we fail to tune in.

TUESDAY — Twenty-Eighth Week of the Year
Rm 1:16-25   *Lk 11:37-41*

First Reading

Paul had spoken of the unity of God's design for the human race. That design is revealed to us in many ways. In today's first reading, Paul describes the breakdown in our human perception of that divine plan. He describes a world without Christ. Without Jesus men and women could know something about God from the world of nature as well as from their own moral experience. Their hearts and minds were darkened, however, and that darkness spread through entire cultures and religions. The religious sense, present in every person, easily became demonic, distorted and deviant. This world, swollen with sin, could not, unaided, attain holiness. Christ not only clarified the nature of God through His teaching, but promised and gave us the power, through the Holy Spirit, to attain holiness. It is the very power of God leading everyone who believes to salvation. The Gospel of Jesus not only shows us what the right track is but enables us to follow that track to come to the same relationship with the Father that He has.

Gospel Reading

This Gospel reading illustrates the distortions that can enter religion. Jesus does not condemn ritual and external observance but insists that the heart of ritual is faith. The heart of the Church and of religious practices is faith. If external observance is the limit of our religion, then sin becomes as superficial as the righteousness that such a faith would seek. The heart of our sacramental life in the Catholic Church is faith. A fruitful participation in the sacraments requires personal faith. The Church survives and thrives by faith: your faith, my faith, our common faith.

Point

Faith brings prayer and ritual to life.

WEDNESDAY — Twenty-Eighth Week of the Year
Rm 2:1-11   *Lk 11:42-46*

First Reading

Paul cautions the Romans not to be too quick to judge those who have done wrong. However culpable others might be, we all are subject to judgment in one way or another. We all have little pockets of hardness in our hearts. The more profoundly and clearly God has revealed Himself to us, the more we are liable and responsible for living in accord with that revelation. Paul phrases this as immortality and glory for those who have followed the light as God has given it to them, and judgment for those who have consciously turned from that light. Paul's caution to us is that we not expend emotional energy in accusation and harsh judgment of others while neglecting the introspection and self-examination that gives birth to a deeper fidelity to God's word in our own lives. God plays no favorites. He judges each person justly but not equally. We are all judged on the basis of what we have been given.

Gospel Reading

In the same fashion, Jesus pronounces special judgment on the Pharisees. It was not that they were more evil than other people. In the vast history of grotesque human behavior, their tiny, mechanical tithing was relatively incidental. It may well have been that conscientious lay people tithed with the same precision. The reason for the Lord's judgment on them is that they should have known better. The Torah Law, prophetic writings and centuries of learning that were available to them should have enabled them to appreciate the priorities in the Law and see that justice and mercy were its central and controlling demands. One has only to skim the prophets to grasp the central thrust of fair-dealing that runs throughout their oracles. The Pharisees failed in this. More was expected of them because more had been given them.

Point

We are all responsible to the Lord for what we have been given.

THURSDAY — Twenty-Eighth Week of the Year
Rm 3:21-29   *Lk 11:47-54*

First Reading

Paul speaks about the sins of pagans and of Jews. Everybody has sinned and fallen short. Therefore, Jesus came and died for all. He did so not because He owed it to us or because the human race had earned it. He died for us from love. It was a gift thoroughly undeserved. All we have to do to be saved is to accept that gift through faith. That's it — the heart of Romans! Justification is by faith alone. Luther interpreted this in one way. He said that all a person needs is faith. When God looks at us, He sees Jesus. Our sinfulness is not thoroughly removed but covered over by the grace of Christ. The Catholic tradition asserts that by faith and the Holy Spirit, we become in fact a new creation. Original sinfulness is not simply covered but removed root and branch. Our prayer and good works, then, have value precisely as expressive of this new birth through Christ and the Holy Spirit. Both traditions have given differing emphasis to the same words of Paul. Gradually, the two positions hardened, different vocabularies developed and different theologies grew out of that original disparity. The Catholic tradition has always emphasized that our manner of life is important not as a bribe to God but as evidence of the extent to which we have made the love of the Trinity part of us.

Gospel Reading

Disparity between status and conduct is what Jesus condemns in today's Gospel reading. The Pharisees laid claim to a holy tradition yet they refused to attend to and in fact, further persecuted those prophets who gave expression to the heart of that tradition. They used their official status to keep people from God and from the liberating experience, even in Old Testament terms, of what it means to be a child of the covenant, chosen and blessed by God.

Point

The works we do expose the inner spirit that animates our life.

FRIDAY — Twenty-Eighth Week of the Year
Rm 4:1-8   Lk 12:1-7

First Reading

In today's first reading, Paul illustrates his previous theological discussion of faith and works by the example of Abraham. Abraham was a holy man justified by God before the Law existed. Therefore, he was justified by his faith. We can step aside briefly from the theology of Romans to apply what Paul is saying to ourselves. Abraham's works (circumcision and sacrifice) had value because they were expressions of his faith. That inner faith made everything he did "faithful." Paul is presenting faith as the functional equivalent of circumcision for Gentiles. The Torah Law and ritual circumcision were simply sacraments of this deeper resident faith that unites a person with God.

Gospel Reading

On the other hand, in today's Gospel reading, Jesus speaks of the yeast of the Pharisees. Their works and observances had little value because they had no faith. There was a vacuum within. Unlike Abraham, that inner emptiness made everything they did — including Torah observance — "faithless." We can use this opportunity to reflect on faith. There is a life cycle to faith. As our body passes through its stages of growth, so does our faith have its "passages." There is the beautiful, almost lyrical faith of the very young; the turbulent, confused faith of the teenager; the background faith of those who are making their mark in the world; the quiet, trusting faith of seniors. There is faith as loyalty and structure for our life; faith as wisdom and calm assurance. Our faith, in short, waxes, wanes, is tested and thrives. It is a living thing that is affected by all the turbulences of our life. Beneath everything else that transpires in our consciousness, faith is the foundation on which we build our value systems, beliefs and philosophy of life.

Point

Like everything else about us, faith has its seasons.

SATURDAY — Twenty-Eighth Week of the Year
Rm 4:13, 16-18   *Lk 12:8-12*

First Reading

Paul's tremendous emphasis on faith was not a theological position arrived at through logical deduction. We cannot isolate Paul's theology from his personal experience. Here was a man who had brutally persecuted the early Christian movement. Suddenly, he had a dramatic experience of the Lord Jesus and of the Lord's love for him. He received the gift of faith. Nothing he had done to that point qualified him for such a gift. It is no surprise, therefore, that Paul generalizes from that experience to a universal principle about faith and salvation. Everything is grace. It is all free! This is one reason why he holds Abraham in such high esteem. Abraham is the premier man of faith. Paul sees Abraham's descendants as comprising all those people of faith through the centuries to whom God has given grace and salvation without their in any way deserving it. This is what Paul views as the true and deep fulfillment of the promise made to Abraham. He was to be the father in faith of millions. They would all be tied together not by genes but by faith.

Gospel Reading

The unforgivable sin against the Holy Spirit is the basic sin against the light. This is the sin for which every person, whether a believer or not, can be liable. Jesus states that those who consciously deny Him before men and do not repent will be denied by Him before the Father in heaven. Those who have argued against Christianity can find forgiveness in God's time under the usual conditions. But this sin against the Spirit in which we deny the very light within us is spiritual and moral suicide, because we asphyxiate our own conscience. Such a sin, by definition, cannot be forgiven.

Point

We can reject all the gifts given us by God and still be forgiven. But to deny our conscience and intellectual ability to recognize truth is the single sin that irreparably destroys our link with God. It is the single, fatal defiance.

MONDAY — Twenty-Ninth Week of the Year
Rm 4:20-25 *Lk 12:13-21*

First Reading

The faith that Paul extolls in Abraham was not an adherence to a set of doctrinal positions but basic trust in God's promises. This posture of fundamental trust is a vital component of faith. Faith is indeed composed of intellectual assent but it also has vital emotional and volitional components. Paul's emphasis is on the reliance Abraham gave to God's promises to him. Trust in the unseen is not easy. The distinction between the kind of faith described by Paul and mere wishful thinking is that faith is grounded on an experience of God. That experience can take many forms: devotional, charismatic, liturgical, ecclesial or historical. That experience provides the base upon which we can look to an undefined future with assurance that God will be with us to carry out His word toward us.

Gospel Reading

Growing rich for oneself as opposed to growing rich in the sight of God is a theme at the heart of all Christian spirituality and specifically the thought of Saint Paul. The issue is often posed as an opposition between professional success and spiritual success. To grow rich in the sight of God is not to empty one's bank account. It is the development of those inner resources and that spiritual strength which enable us to appreciate God's love for us and the presence of His care throughout our lives. That inner strength becomes a rock on which lives can be built. On that foundation, we can proceed to live our social and professional lives. To amass wealth for oneself is, as seen in today's Gospel parable, to accumulate a hoard of possessions and contacts without any central moral or spiritual base upon which they can be rested. We become slaves of our possessions. Should they disappear, we have nothing else to rely upon. Wealth for oneself is essentially a kind of spiritual bankruptcy.

Point

Trust in God orients our attitude toward our world. It determines whether we see the world as an essentially hostile place or basically a home.

TUESDAY — Twenty-Ninth Week of the Year

Rm 5:12, 15, 17-19, 20-21   *Lk 12:35-38*

First Reading

Adam and Christ provide the polar points of Paul's argument in today's first reading. Adam was the vehicle for the entry of sin into the world. Paul speaks here in terms of corporate personality. To the extent that we are like Adam in our human and physical composition, the sin that emerged from his psycho-physical structure is also endemic in our own. As Adam sinned, we all have sinned. The other pole of the argument is Jesus Christ. Just as Jesus gave a new, dynamic and Godward orientation to humanity, so to the extent that we are incorporated into Christ, we become capable of that same orientation. Hence, grace became a human possibility through the Incarnation and Resurrection of Christ. If sin is pervasive throughout the world, so the grace of Christ can pervade the world as well. The life, death and Resurrection of Christ showed that grace is more powerful and binding than sin. Grace is the signal of God's victory over sin and death. That victory can be ours.

Gospel Reading

Vigilance for the Lord's return is characteristic of the posture of His disciples. Between the first and second comings of Christ is an interim period demanding great faith, spiritual strength and communal support. Waiting for the Lord's return requires an attentiveness to details of the spiritual life. During this period of the Church, we have been given a variety of aids to help us remain watchful not only for the Lord's final return in glory but for His presence to us in power however and whenever that may come. We have been given the Scriptures, the liturgy, our communal life and a host of religious aids to enable us to keep alive to the Lord's presence. Our faith during this time of waiting and sacramental signs is the real test of faithful discipleship.

Point

The patient endurance that was Christ's can be ours as well through His grace.

WEDNESDAY — Twenty-Ninth Week of the Year
Rm 6:12-18   *Lk 12:39-48*

First Reading

In today's first reading, Paul speaks about the power of sin. He refers not simply to individual acts but to sin as though it were a foreign power or virus inside us with its own momentum which we cannot control. Even though we are baptized into the Lord Jesus, the residual effects of the extracted power of sin remain in us. They are somewhat like the phantom feelings that remain when a limb is removed. The battle between sin and grace continues in our bodies and lives. Much like a habit that we think we have under control, we find that it surfaces again when we least expect it. We are constantly reminded of the holding power of sin. Baptism does not immunize us from those residual effects. For this reason, our prayer life and spiritual life need constant attention not only because old tendencies tend to resurface but also because special moments of grace-filled revelation can come unexpectedly as well.

Gospel Reading

The unexpected and sacred moments of reconciliation and prayer come without our necessarily anticipating them. The Lord comes to us unexpectedly even in crisis. That is the subject of today's Gospel reading. It really is a warning against complacency. Such an admonition is necessary not because the Holy Spirit is weak but because, unlike the Lord Jesus, we are not completely transparent to God's power. We have pockets of resistance in our lives. That is the reason why we become a battleground and a place of struggle.

Point

The fact that we experience the struggle of the spiritual life is not a sign of failure but of success. Those who are totally closed to God's Spirit have given up the struggle.

THURSDAY — Twenty-Ninth Week of the Year
Rm 6:19-23   *Lk 12:49-53*

First Reading

Although Paul speaks about slavery, his point in today's first reading becomes clearer to us if we speak about an employer-employee relationship. Paul compares the old life of sin and the new life of grace in terms of servitude. When we were "employed" by sin, we used all our abilities, talents and capacities to serve that employer. The result? We were paid with spiritual death. The effects of sin in human affairs are too dismal to need constant rehearsing. The world in which we live is the best evidence of the effects of sin in human life. When we are "employed" by God, our wages are life, freedom and an eternal existence with the Lord. Here and there in our world, we can see islands of human concern and peace that are the best evidence of what life in God's presence can be like. Even if we take a very practical cost-benefit analysis of the spiritual life, we come to the conclusion that our best short-term and long-range interests are served by service of God rather than of sin.

Gospel Reading

The division of which the Lord speaks in today's Gospel reading is not simply generational or familial. That is indeed what it might have been in the early Gentile Church to which Luke is writing. But the division cuts across all lines. The zeal that Jesus would enkindle is one that does not start wars but which spotlights the sin from which it has turned. People of great holiness do not intrinsically desire to create conflict. Their disparate behavior from those whose lives are not guided by grace, and the reaction they thereby generate, create conflict and strife. Nothing can so upset and disorient a community of thieves as one honest person. Few things can so rip apart a group of perjurers as one individual who insists on telling the truth. This is the strife of which Jesus speaks. It is the kind of reactive strife that we see exhibited in His own life.

Point

Servants of sin and servants of God both receive an appropriate wage.

FRIDAY — Twenty-Ninth Week of the Year
Rm 7:18-25   *Lk 12:54-59*

First Reading

This is a famous passage from Paul's letter to the Romans. He describes a conflict that we all experience at some point in our lives. The good we want to do, we do not end up doing. In fact, we end up doing the very opposite of what we know to be right. Knowing the right thing to do is not enough. The drives within us are much deeper and more consuming than our intellectual conclusions. Paul asks who can release us from this slavery. The answer is found in the Lord through His Holy Spirit. This internal conflict can take many forms. It can show itself through lust, greed, and the thirst for power. If we expand this intrinsic conflict in ourselves to the entire world, we can see the cause of world tension. The conflict between good and evil deep within the human soul underlies the economic and political tensions in our world.

Gospel Reading

This cosmic conflict will continue until the end of our world. In today's Gospel reading, Jesus speaks about the signs of the times. We know how to recognize the signs of changing weather. We cannot yet change climate. All we can do is prepare for the change. But when it comes to conflicts within our own life, between individuals, we are able to bring some measure of peace and settlement. We can bring repose and reconciliation between ourselves and those around us. When we examine the great national issues of racism, nuclear war, economic injustice and communism we should not forget the equally important and infinitely more manageable conflicts in our own life to which we can bring some peace.

Point

Bringing reconciliation into our corner of the world is a small but real contribution to the resolution of the cosmic battle between good and evil.

SATURDAY — Twenty-Ninth Week of the Year
Rm 8:1-11   *Lk 13:1-9*

First Reading

The word "law" occurs in today's first reading in a variety of senses. Paul speaks about the law of the Spirit and the law of sin. Here, he refers to rule-directed or oriented behavior. We do not move randomly from one thing to another. However antinomian and free we might think ourselves to be, our actions are governed by rules — often subconscious and implicit. Our life exhibits a philosophy of life and an orientation. The critical issue is to determine the direction of that orientation. Paul speaks, therefore, about an orientation toward sin or toward the Spirit of Christ. Each of these has its own dynamic which eventuates in its own result. If we submit ourselves to the "law" of sin, we will discover that, despite occasional flashes of good will, our overall tendency is toward spiritual and personal death. If we submit ourselves to the "law" of Christ's Spirit, then our overall tendency will be lifeward despite occasional failings. Between these meanings of "law," Paul inserts the traditional meaning of Law as Torah. When people were oriented by the "law" of sin, the Torah was powerless to assist them. It gave rules that nobody could obey. Now, when we are oriented by the "law" of the Spirit, the Torah finds a deeper and more significant fulfillment than was ever possible before.

Gospel Reading

Jesus refers in this important passage to the apparently accidental death of eighteen people beneath a fallen tower. He states that such a horrible death did not imply that they were greater sinners than anyone else. We cannot correlate material success or failure with grace or sin so easily. The Lord states that those who do not repent will experience a more terrible spiritual death. Spiritual collapse is more death-dealing than physical death because its implications are eternal. The Lord then gives us a comforting image of a fruitless tree. There is always time to change until the final harvest. At that time, we are stuck with what we have done and left undone. Until that point, however, there is always time to find a fresh direction for our life.

Point

We can allow our lives to follow their inertial tendency toward sin or we can consciously direct them toward God. In either case, we are responsible for what we will have become.

MONDAY — Thirtieth Week of the Year
Rm 8:12-17   *Lk 13:10-17*

First Reading

Paul states that we are all debtors, but not to the flesh. The word "flesh" (sarx) for Paul has a very technical meaning. He does not mean that the body is evil. By the "flesh" Paul refers to the entire person — mind, emotions, will and body — without the Holy Spirit. He is speaking in this reading about the spiritual life. He says, in effect, that now that we have received the Holy Spirit, we are not compelled to do what our old sinful self would want us to do. We have received a new principle of life which not only places us in a new relationship with God but also gives us new power. We are no longer slaves but sons and daughters of God. This means that now we have a right and a claim to His gifts. "Father" is not simply a traditional name attributed to God. It is a way of experiencing God.

Gospel Reading

Today's Gospel reading highlights a point that complements Paul's statements. The Lord's healing of the long-ailing woman shows that sin is not a local thing. In the Gospels, all sorts of ailments that we call secular or medical are attributed to sin. In a sense, in all of His healings Jesus is dealing directly or indirectly with the effects of sin. Sin is not in the brain, liver or pancreas. It is a factor that pervades a person's entire being. In the same way, the Holy Spirit is not a thing located in our heart, brain or spleen. He pervades our entire personality. To live as a son or daughter of God is to live out the consequences of that Spirit inside us. It takes a great deal of spiritual discipline to unlock that Spirit we have all received. It takes courage to allow that Spirit to spill out into all the areas of our life.

Point

The central issue of Christian growth is not possession of the Holy Spirit but surrender to Him.

TUESDAY — Thirtieth Week of the Year
Rm 8:18-25   *Lk 13:18-21*

First Reading

Yesterday, Paul spoke about the Spirit of adoption that we have all received in baptism. Today, we read about events in our newspapers and wonder how the two can be reconciled.

The world is indeed in labor as we try to give birth to that Spirit within us. What Jesus did in handing over His Spirit was not simply to save souls but to set in motion the transformation of creation. He came to bring a new heaven and a new earth. Jesus Christ in His risen glory is the goal of everything — economics, politics, prayer. That glory toward which we are slowly moving and the suffering we experience now are connected. The world has been distorted by centuries of sin. To change direction involves pain. It is very much like the effort to end a long-ingrained habit of smoking or drinking. It is also like the pain of giving birth. We are all giving birth to this new creation. We are its midwives.

Gospel Reading

Jesus did not come just to establish a Church. He came to bring all people into the kingdom. He formed a community as a vehicle for that primary goal. In today's Gospel reading, the Lord speaks about the mustard seed that starts very small in size. Luke emphasizes its eventual global embrace. Just as yeast "influences" dough, so the kingdom will eventually permeate the world. This does not mean that the entire world will become Roman Catholic — at least not in the sense in which we presently know it. It does mean that all people will be influenced by the presence of the kingdom.

Point

The pain of the world is condensed in us as we give birth to the new creation.

WEDNESDAY — Thirtieth Week of the Year
Rm 8:26-30   *Lk 13:22-30*

First Reading

Paul had spoken about the Holy Spirit we have all received and the labor we endure to allow that Spirit to fill our lives. In this reading, he emphasizes the fact that the same Spirit helps us in our weakness. All the groaning, pain and exasperation we experience can become a prayer! Prayer need not be in words. Whatever raises our hearts and minds to God is prayer. The Spirit within us can turn our suffering into prayer. In the last analysis, God makes all things work out for good. Paul's reference is not necessarily to material or financial good but always to spiritual good. Paradoxically, a divorce, the death of a loved one, cancer or bankruptcy can draw forth the Spirit from within us. Finally, Paul's reference to "predestination" is chock full of heretical potential. Too long a reflection on predestination can drive a person crazy. It is best not to start down that road from which one will never come back psychologically intact. We can simply say that Paul's meaning is that God does not do things on the spur of the moment. Everything fits into a larger design in which each of us is included.

Gospel Reading

The Lord tells us in today's Gospel reading that our baptism and reception of the Holy Spirit is only a beginning. It begins the process of our striving to enter by the narrow door. Through Jesus a magnificent and marvelous eternal life is ours that we can only begin to glimpse here. Many things surround us to deflect us from the way. If we maintain faith, God will use even these temptations to fulfill the destiny that He intends for each of us.

Point

The Spirit can turn what seems to be a failure into a stupendous spiritual opportunity.

THURSDAY — Thirtieth Week of the Year
Rm 8:31-39   *Lk 13:31-35*

First Reading

Paul concludes this section of the letter to the Romans about the interior presence of the Holy Spirit. This Spirit links us to God. After all of Paul's magnificent reflections, we should remember that he is describing baptism — not ordination or episcopal consecration. Baptism is the primordial sacrament. It is our basic spiritual credit card. All other sacraments are built upon it. In today's reading, Paul emphasizes that the significance of all this is that God is on our side. God is with us. We know this because Christ died for us. From this point, nobody should feel they are not worthy. We are lovable and loved. Also, no person can take our baptism away from us. There is no spell, no curse, no aggressor, no ban of excommunication, no clerical suspension that can take away that trace of the Holy Spirit that we call baptismal character. It is with us forever as an indelible sign of either what we are or what we could have been.

Gospel Reading

One detail stands out in today's Gospel reading. Not all Pharisees were hostile to Jesus. Jerusalem was a symbol of political and ecclesiastical power. Jesus did not reject Jerusalem. Jerusalem cut itself off from Him. Very soon, Jesus would make His last appeal to Jerusalem on Palm Sunday. It will be then that official Jerusalem will show its true colors. It would write itself out of the Book of Life.

Point

With all the changes and emotional oscillations in our lives, God remains on our side. His love for us is not a variable but a constant.

FRIDAY — Thirtieth Week of the Year
Rm 9:1-5   *Lk 14:1-6*

First Reading

The mystery that preoccupied and fascinated Paul was the status of the Israelites, the Jewish people. In this section of the letter to the Romans, he explores the meaning of the old covenant and of their rejection of the Lord. Himself a loyal Jew until his conversion and probably afterward in his own way, Paul was haunted throughout his apostolate by the question of the relationship between the new covenant grace of Christ and the old covenant law. At times, in flights of rhetoric, he depreciates the old law and covenant almost to the point of worthlessness. That was simply rhetorical exaggeration. The old covenant remains God's special bond with the Jewish people today. Paul examines its theological implications and emphasizes the glory that belongs to the Jewish people: covenant, law, liturgy. He is puzzled by the question of what went wrong.

Gospel Reading

Part of what went wrong is clear in today's Gospel reading. The great theological themes of the covenant became legalized and politicized. Excessive preoccupation with law had sucked the spiritual lift and drive out of observance of the old covenant. This of itself did not make that covenant invalid. What it did was to provide the basis for the new covenant in Jesus' blood. The preaching of the early Church as remembered for us in the New Testament would be formed largely through reaction against the narrowmindedness and legalism of the old law. For the early Christian community, the old covenant and its excessively legalistic interpretation became a negative norm. This was especially the case in the Gentile churches founded by Paul.

Point

*The Jewish people remains chosen for a special relation-
ship with God and with the Christian community. We share the
same Father if not the same Messiah.*

SATURDAY — Thirtieth Week of the Year
Rm 11:1-2, 11-12, 25-29　　　　　　　　　　*Lk 14:1, 7-11*

First Reading

Paul's struggle with the place of the Jewish people in
God's design continues. He makes several important assertions
in today's first reading that should put Christian anti-Semitism
forever to rest. God has not rejected the Jewish people. His
promises and love for them remain as vivid as in David's time.
Their rejection of the Lord Jesus as Messiah does not mean that
they are condemned. Their rejection of the Gospel provided
the trigger for the evangelization of Gentiles, which caused the
rapid growth in the number of Christians. Paul remarks that
somehow in God's providence their fidelity to their covenant
with God will bring them salvation. Of course, they cannot
know the fullness of life that we have in Jesus through His Holy
Spirit. The non-baptized can experience God's love but in a
fashion that will always be extraordinary. The ordinary experience of Christians is the extraordinary privilege of some of the
non-baptized. The Jewish experience of God will be measured
by that of the anawim — by faithful waiting and reliance on the
promise. They await what the Christian is able to experience
now.

Gospel Reading

Our Christian posture toward the Jews is not one of antipathy but of brotherhood. The message of Jesus' words in

today's Gospel reading is that there is no place in the kingdom for spiritual self-exaltation. He is not simply giving instructions for table etiquette. He is making a profoundly spiritual point. Spiritual hubris is self-destructive. Those who gloat over their special entry to God and who deprecate their neighbor's spiritual vitality are in fact negating the very thing they claim to have. The attitude of the Christian community toward other religious traditions should not be measured in terms of superiority but of service. Our special intimacy with the Lord should enable us to assist and not deprecate the spiritual journey of others.

Point

Our closeness to the Lord is measured by how close we are to those around us.

MONDAY — Thirty-First Week of the Year
Rm 11:29-36   *Lk 14:12-14*

First Reading

We come to the end of Paul's discussion of the place of the Jewish people in the economy of salvation. He asserts that the Jews have not been rejected by God, are still the chosen people and eventually will be saved. The old covenant has not been abrogated. Paul is insistent that the Roman Christians, who were largely non-Jewish, have received the Gospel message and the grace of Christ precisely because the Jews rejected Jesus. God's design works in ways that are inscrutable to us. Even though the Jewish people rejected the Gospel, God is not finished with them. He still invites them to share in the new covenant. So many people we know seem to have rejected God and turned their backs on the Church. We should re-member that God is not finished with them. They still experience the twitch of God's grace at some point in their lives. The books are not closed on anyone until the moment of death.

Gospel Reading

On one level, the Lord speaks about the kingdom. He describes those who are invited. It is not just people who are "together" spiritually. The kingdom is not a ghetto. Everyone is invited in. The further point that Jesus makes to us is that Christian service and concern must not be a subtle disguise for enhancing our reputation. The more genuine our service to others is, the more effective a vehicle it will be for God's grace to them. It is not a voice from heaven but our ordinary dealings with others that in some mysterious way can be what brings people back to the Lord.

Point

However publicly someone may seem to have rejected the Lord, that refusal is never final.

TUESDAY — Thirty-First Week of the Year
Rm 12:5-15   *Lk 14:15-24*

First Reading

Paul's image of the Church as the Body of Christ is a classic one. Its import is a refusal to insist on a dead uniformity in Church membership. We all have gifts that can be used both to preach the Gospel in various ways to others, and to enhance the faith that people already possess. We all have abilities that can be used to deepen community spirit and the intensity of our common experience of the Lord. Paul speaks of the gifts of prophecy, exhortation, teaching, administration and generosity — the ability to help with time or money. These very differences make the Body of Christ a dynamic entity that is not static but a growing, thriving community. These gifts must be encouraged, assembled and coordinated. All Christians are obliged to enable each other to realize that every person is an integral and important part of the Church. The different members of the Body are not to be ranked in order of importance but in order of function. We are all functionally interrelated. There are no super-Christians among us. We all contribute to the community Jesus founded.

Gospel Reading

Invitations can be refused in all kinds of ways. The first level of meaning in today's parable is that of the Jewish people who refused entry into the kingdom as offered by Christ. On a second level, the reference is to Christians who refuse to share the gifts they have with the parish at large. The Lord asks us to give not the crumbs from our table but our very substance to our fellow-Christians with whom we share a common baptism. That substance is not necessarily financial. It is the aggregate of talents, viewpoints, abilities and experiences we have accumulated. All of these can be used to bring the kingdom into greater public reality.

Point

The Lord invites us to share not only what we have but what we are with the community of faith to which we belong.

WEDNESDAY — Thirty-First Week of the Year
Rm 13:8-10   *Lk 14:25-33*

First Reading

This section of Paul's letter to the Romans follows his

exposition of a number of profound theological themes. Here he is summing up with a series of exhortations aimed at the Church at Rome. His subject in today's reading is love. The statement that we should owe no debt to another except that of love is deceptively simple. In fact, a debt of love has far-reaching consequences. To have an obligation of love requires a commitment and concern for the well-being of people to whom we are not related, that goes far beyond any legal obligation. Throughout Romans, Paul has spoken of our freedom from the Torah Law and the free grace we have received in Christ. Here, he replaces the Torah Law with an obligation more binding and thorough than anything that might have been interpreted of the Torah by a scholarly rabbi. The range of love is wide and free. It varies with circumstance, age, place and culture. But it is the fulfillment of the Law.

Gospel Reading

The obligation to love is also the indirect subject of the Lord's words in today's Gospel reading. Jesus speaks about discipleship. He instructs us to make a careful and intelligent examination of the demands of authentic discipleship. To turn one's back on father and mother is a graphic way of illustrating the totality of commitment required by the Lord. Careful planning is part of a serious effort to follow. One can be a disciple in name and phrase. But a serious effort to examine what it means to follow Christ, what love requires, how we give expression to the Gospel message in an urban or suburban society is not susceptible to a series of quick and facile clichés. Each person has to give serious consideration as to how he or she will incarnate their baptismal spirit in their lives. That is the kind of thoughtful deliberation for which the Lord calls.

Point

Faith can be expressed in various trivial and unsatisfying ways. It can also be a radical and penetrating way of living with depth and satisfaction.

THURSDAY — Thirty-First Week of the Year
Rm 14:7-12   *Lk 15:1-10*

First Reading

This puzzling first reading comes out of a larger section. Paul has spoken about Christ as the axis of our spiritual life. Here, he draws some practical conclusions. The Roman Christians were a mix of people. A few kept old Jewish practices and others either stopped doing so or never did in the first place. Paul tells them not to judge each other. We should not judge because each of us is trying in his or her own way to serve the Lord Jesus. None of us is living for himself or herself. The way we live is for the Lord and the way we die is for the Lord. Instead of engaging in judgmental analyses, we should assist and support each other and not hinder individual, though highly idiosyncratic, efforts to live out the Gospel.

Gospel Reading

The fact that tax collectors and public sinners were drawing near to Jesus meant, to the scribes, that something was radically wrong here. The outcasts followed Jesus because He told them about a God who cared for them. In Jesus, God reached out to the lost and excluded sheep. Jesus did not show them a God who insists that they purify themselves and only come to Him when they were clean and perfected. Rather, He told them of a God who remains close even when we fall. Even if a person is contemplating suicide, the Spirit of God within him still calls him back from the brink. Jesus did not tell them about a God on the mountain to whom we climb on our knees, but a God who comes down to us searching through thorns and bushes for those who are lost. This is one difference between Jesus and the Pharisees. They represented a God who demanded that we be healed before we enter His presence. Jesus told of a God who came to heal.

Point

Enough forces work in the world to divide us. The community of Jesus must spend its energy to unite people.

FRIDAY — Thirty-First Week of the Year
Rm 15:14-21   *Lk 16:1-8*

First Reading

In this first reading, Paul speaks about his ministry and work for the Lord. "I am convinced you are filled with goodness." This entire letter was written as a reminder of the things which the Roman Christians knew deep within their souls. We all need such reminders because it is very easy to fall into a spiritual rut. The function of a homily is to remind us of dimensions of faith that we may have forgotten or selectively dismissed from our consciousness. A homilist presents us with a vision of the spiritual world wider than what we may have been able to experience to date. This was Paul's message to the Romans. He stated a truth in stark terms to drive its message home. God loves us no matter what we do. We cannot earn His love. It is a free gift.

Gospel Reading

The function of Gospel parables is also to strike us with the religious dimensions of ordinary experience. Jesus takes homely scenes from everyday life and finds within them a lesson or point to make about the spiritual dimension of life and the kingdom in which we are called to share. Today's parable speaks not about the steward's dishonesty but about his genius in planning for his own future. The Lord's remark is that we should be as enterprising when it comes to exploiting spiritual opportunities in our own life. Just as we have to learn to deal wisely with our financial affairs, car repairs, career and family life, so in similar fashion, we have to learn to deal creatively and maturely with the Holy Spirit that we have received. Intelligent planning in things sacred and secular is the mark of spiritual and secular adulthood.

Point

We are not called to remain in childhood innocence but to grow into spiritual adulthood. That growth comes through the strain of life and the experience of sin — ours and that of others.

SATURDAY — Thirty-First Week of the Year
Rm 16:3-9, 16, 22-27   *Lk 16:9-15*

First Reading

Paul concludes his letter to the Romans with a litany of greetings and thanks to all the people who made his ministry possible. It can happen that in reading of Paul's adventures and successes, we can forget that he was simply the center of a vast network of co-workers who assisted him in his work. When we read about great modern day Christians such as Pope John Paul II and Mother Teresa as well as other great heroes, we should recall the enormous number of unnamed people who have spent time, effort and money to enable them to do their work. These staff people and support personnel are important to their ministry. They enable these great individuals to exercise the specific gift they have been given. The same is true in any parish. For the few names that are widely known, there are many others who fold chairs, clean the church, iron linens, fix lights, and run societies. They enable a parish to be an effective expression of the Body of Christ.

Gospel Reading

The choice is stark: God or mammon. Each of us has a god we serve. The question centers upon which will attract our devotion. Jesus tells us to make friends through our use of this world's goods. It is a reminder that the spiritual bonds of human friendship are more important than the simple accumulation of things. Spiritual bonds endure over time. Things can be lost and can rot. We should use the time and opportunities we have to widen our friendships and attach ourselves to a community that will place us into a wider and more enduring context of meaning than our own narrow self-interest. There are a variety of ways of achieving that. Parish service is one of the most prominent.

Point

We should use things we have to enhance our friendships and not use our friendships to enhance the number of things we have.

MONDAY — Thirty-Second Week of the Year
Ws 1:1-7   *Lk 17:1-6*

First Reading

The Book of Wisdom, or the Wisdom of Solomon, is part of the Old Testament wisdom tradition which includes Proverbs, Ecclesiastes, Sirach and the stories of Judith, Esther and Tobit. This book was written in Greek about a century before Christ. It expresses the Old Testament experience of God in terms of Greek philosophical principles. It was written for Jews living in Egypt. There were different strands in the wisdom tradition. This book was written to counteract the viewpoint of Ecclesiastes which had said that life was short and without hope ("turn, turn, turn"). Today's reading shows that God saves the righteous, that is, those who seek after Him. The reading is emphatic that the search for God and our experience of Him do not occur in the abstract. They grow from the kind of life we live. A sense of God emerges from a life rightly lived. This reverses the usual order in which we claim that belief affects life. Wisdom asserts that the kind of life we live affects our belief. If one engages in fair dealing with others, God is experienced with greater force and power.

Gospel Reading

If we read today's reading in the context of a community of people trying to be sensitive to the Lord's presence, we can appreciate their horror of scandal and their need for frequent forgiveness to neutralize the acid of resentment. We can see, as well, the power faith has to hold a community of separate individuals together. We cannot isolate the quality and intensity of our personal faith from the kind of community in which we live and the kind of life we lead.

Point

As we try to live the Gospel ideal, the more vivid will the Lord be to us.

TUESDAY — Thirty-Second Week of the Year
Ws 2:23-3:9   *Lk 17:7-10*

First Reading

This first reading is part of a larger commentary on the Book of Genesis from the Book of Wisdom. Two points stand out in this reading. First, the measure of life is not a materialistic one. If we do not restrain what we eat and drink, for example, five years can take an enormous toll on our health. The measure of a successful life is intangible. It is determined by our relationships with others and the peace we can maintain within. Further, the evidence of a successful life is not limited to the number of chronological years we have. We live on a larger stage. An inability to find a date for the junior prom in high school does not mean that we are a failure. To fail an examination does not imply that we have failed the test of life. If a person succeeds financially or professionally, that does not mean that he or she has been successful in achieving God's design for them. Commercial failure or success is not identical with spiritual failure or success.

Gospel Reading

Jesus' message to us in today's Gospel reading is that living in the light of the hard spiritual realities of God's judgment is not an extraordinary achievement that somehow places God in our debt. We are not doing Him a favor. We are simply recognizing reality. We are doing our duty. The gift of eternal life in God's presence which we have through Jesus Christ is not given to us for unusual heroism. It is given for our simply remaining faithful.

Point

Doing our best is expected of every Christian.

WEDNESDAY — Thirty-Second Week of the Year
Ws 6:2-11   *Lk 17:11-19*

First Reading

Today's first reading speaks about God's terrible swift sword. It is a warning to those in authority both in civil and ecclesiastical positions of power. They will be judged by a higher standard than the people over whom they minister. People in authority stand in the privileged position of wielding enormous authority over others. In effect, they stand in the place of God. People almost instinctively want to trust their spiritual and civil authorities. When that authority is abused or incorrectly used, the sin is a double one. It involves not only personal infidelity but the corrosion of trust in institutions. Corruption, whether in Church or State, is especially horrendous because it eats away at the institutional foundations of life. The sins of any authority figure call for a special vengeance because they are sins not only against God but against the social arrangements into which God has entrusted His authority. It is a sin against the people as a whole.

Gospel Reading

Ten were cleansed but only the Samaritan returned to give thanks. This episode anticipates the later success which the early Church would have in evangelizing the Samaritans. More broadly, however, it is a story of human prayer in need and our forgetfulness when prayer is granted. Many of us have made rash promises like vowing to pray a hundred rosaries if a particular petition is granted. Did we do this when our prayer was answered? This is one reason for the Church's strong insistence on the regular celebration of the Eucharist. It reminds us to give thanks at all seasons of our life. It is an occasion for us to be reminded of the essential giftedness of our life.

Point

When we are specially positioned as holders of power or recipients of grace, we have an unusual obligation to be aware of God's presence in those special, almost sacramental, moments.

THURSDAY — Thirty-Second Week of the Year
Ws 7:22-8:1   *Lk 17:20-25*

First Reading

This first reading is a personification of wisdom. To the Greeks, personification was a way of emphasizing the importance of wisdom as a kind of world-soul (Logos) that pervades all things. The wisdom that fills the universe is an expression of God. It is a Greek contribution to our theology. It was a vehicle for showing the pervasive omnipresence of God without detracting from His transcendence. It later provided a way of conceptualizing the Holy Spirit. The pervasive presence of God in individuals as well as in the structure of the universe is through the Spirit. It is a presence that is so intrinsic to the structure of human intelligence and natural reality as to be empirically invisible. The kingdom of which the Lord speaks is the public acknowledgment of that presence.

Gospel Reading

The arrival of that kingdom is the subject of today's Gospel reading. The Lord tells us that the kingdom will not arrive with visible signs which we can watch, as so many apocalyptic newsletters assert. One cannot say to a neutral observer that the kingdom is localized in one spot over another. It is not identical with political or economic systems. It is a reality within us and in our world silently and slowly at work. Jesus warns us not to pay attention to those who want to localize, package and institutionalize it. When the day of final revelation comes, the kingdom's pervasive presence will be obvious to all. It will be as clear as lightning on a stormy night. However, just as the Lord had to suffer before His day of glory, so the Church must endure a great deal before the glory of the reign of God appears. For now, the Church is only an anticipatory sign, an early signal, of what that kingdom can be. Any further effort to concretize and finalize it is bound to fail.

Point

Amid all the apocalyptic speculation of our time, we should remember that we do not need to witness the apocalypse to experience salvation.

FRIDAY — Thirty-Second Week of the Year
Ws 13:1-9   *Lk 17:26-37*

First Reading

This first reading is not an argument for God's existence from creation to Creator. It is about idolatry. When people worship idols of any kind, they fail to go to the source. Idolatry is essentially to take a manifestation of God as the Real Thing. This argument is unusual because Israel classically moved from her historical experience to a notion of God. Through the events of her history, as interpreted by the prophets, she came to see God as Liberator, Savior and Judge. The Greek philosophers moved, not from history, but from the natural features of the world to a notion of God. The result was an abstract, bloodless, cold God packed with pure perfections. To avoid making God too abstract a theorem, we should connect

Him with our own experience and see Him as purposively operative not only in history but in our own lives.

Gospel Reading

This is a difficult Gospel reading. The Lord refers to popular indifference about our final end similar to that of people at the time of Noah and Lot. The parables of Jesus indicate that there would be an undetermined lapse of time before His return. When that decisive moment comes, however, each person will be on his or her own. Where the carcasses are, there will be the vultures. Where human beings exist, even in remote sections of the planet, there will judgment occur. There is no escaping personal accountability. In all of these apocalyptic statements of the Lord, three levels are operative. There is reference to the destruction of Jerusalem, the end of the cosmic world and our individual end at death. The difficulty in our understanding Jesus' assertions about the end is that the evangelists crammed all three levels together. They are difficult for us to unravel. Unlike the Greek gods, our God is involved in our lives. There will come a time when He will bring us to a moment of fulfillment in an historical event that signals the end of an era, or in the final end of history, or in our own death in its normal course.

Point

At the "end," we should be prepared to answer whether we have done our best in using the gifts and opportunities the Lord has given us.

SATURDAY — Thirty-Second Week of the Year
Ws 18:14-16; 19:6-9   *Lk 18:1-8*

First Reading

This magnificent reading, with which we are familiar from

the Christmas liturgy, is part of a deep meditation on the Book of Exodus. It describes God's mighty Word leaping down in prophetic judgment against Egypt but full of grace for Israel. He led the Israelites from the plague-punished land through the Red Sea into the place of promise. This reflection sees the Word at work through all the secondary causes that filled the Exodus event. That Word would have a subsequent history through the prophets until, finally, He would become flesh and blood in Bethlehem. Just as the Word was a word of judgment and of grace at the time of the Exodus, so was the Word made flesh a word of grace and judgment in Galilee and Jerusalem. That same Word is a word of grace and judgment today as at the end of time.

Gospel Reading

Luke uses Jesus's image of the reluctant judge not to show the efficacy of persistent prayer but the fulfillment of God's justice. The widow's prayer for her right moves even the corrupt judge to decide in her favor. A fortiori, God will bring judgment when He comes at the end to bring justice to the face of the earth. There will be no escaping that majestic moment. It will be a time when all that is wrong will be forever set right. The last remark of the Lord is a commentary on the state of affairs among mankind. The lack of justice in ordinary affairs is a great test of our faith. The lack of equity is a great trial for God's people. Jesus asks how long their faith can hold on in the face of persistent and recurrent injustice. He asks rhetorically whether any faith will be left on the face of the earth when He returns to set things right. This interim period is a great test. For that reason, the search for justice is at the same time a way of keeping faith.

Point

At the end of time, the ancient and ever-new Word of God comes again as a Word of grace and judgment.

MONDAY — Thirty-Third Week of the Year
1 M 1:10-15, 41-43, 54-57, 62-63   *Lk 18:35-43*

First Reading

The Book of Maccabees describes the Jewish resistance against Syria. It was written about a century before Christ to portray events that took place a half century before that. Let us set the scene. The Persians allowed the Jews to return to Jerusalem at the time of Ezra and Nehemiah. Only a minority went back as the rest remained scattered all over the Mediterranean. This minority rebuilt the city and Temple and were more strict and orthodox than Jews in other parts of the world. Today's reading refers to those who wanted to propagate Greek culture among the returned Jews. They were called "breakers of the Law." In their effort to fit in with the surrounding cultural trends, they went to the gymnasium (a sort of Greek country club), covered up their circumcision marks and paid little attention to the "abomination of desolation" statue. This week, we will read the story of the resistance of loyal, orthodox Jews to all this. It is a story of old-fashioned heroism. It raises the question for us whether there is anything in our life for which we are willing to die. This story is read during the Thanksgiving and Christmas seasons which are times of strong traditions. We might examine what there is in our life that is so central to our identity as to be non-negotiable.

Gospel Reading

The cure of the blind man speaks not only of the restoration of physical sight but of the gradual emergence of spiritual sight among the disciples. We can take this time of the year to refocus on Jesus Christ as we take a fresh look at ourselves and our traditions. It is important that we not simply view our customs from the outside but from the inside — that is, with the eyes of faith. Religious traditions are not optional eccentricities that one is free to adopt. Our growth within a tradition means that our tradition very much defines who and what we are. Nobody is outside a tradition. It makes us part of a larger whole.

Point

Not only individuals but community traditions are vehicles of the Holy Spirit.

TUESDAY — Thirty-Third Week of the Year
2 M 6:18-31 *Lk 19:1-10*

First Reading

For the early Christians, this story of old Eleazar provided a model of martyrdom. He refused to violate the levitical law by eating pork. His associates questioned what difference a little pork could make. If he pretended to eat the pork, he could survive another day to fight against the system. They were seeking a way out of this dilemma. He could "ingest" the pork without really "eating" it. Eleazar was old-fashioned and stood his ground on principle for two reasons. First, the abstinence from pork was a symbol of his Jewishness. It was a question of authenticity. As a Jew, there were certain things he would not do. Secondly, he was concerned about the example he gave to the younger generation. His private faith had public effects. He felt an obligation to his ancestors as well as to his descendants and would not appear to compromise and thereby scandalize the younger people whose identity as Jews was still fragile.

Gospel Reading

Evidently, Zacchaeus drew the line differently than did Eleazar. Zacchaeus' profession had fraud built into it. He was the managing tax collector in Jericho, a wealthy town filled with quite a few Jewish priests. He was not an evil man. His meeting with the Lord Jesus changed him so that he resolved to give half his profits to the poor and to compensate those he had defrauded with quadruple damages. Jesus calls him a true son of Abraham. Eleazar and Zacchaeus again raise the question for us as to what things we represent to others. What are the guiding principles of our lives? Are we guided by principle or by a series of convenient, disconnected ad-hoc compromises? Eleazar and Zacchaeus had beliefs at the core of their lives. We might examine what the fixed points of our lives might and should be.

Point

If we find that fixed points exist in our life, the next question is whether they center on the Lord Jesus.

WEDNESDAY — Thirty-Third Week of the Year
2 M 7:1, 20-31   Lk 19:11-28

First Reading

Again, in this first reading, we have a heroic and old-fashioned story. The king continues to peddle his pork. He promises to make this family rich and happy if the members abandon their traditions. They see fidelity as an obligation not only toward God but also toward the community. Although there were a set of easy justifications available, they refused to take this path. They were devoted not to an abstract principle such as "Judaism" but to a concrete community. These traditions which they would not depart from or betray, linked them with the past and with the future.

Gospel Reading

This parable was intended for those who believed the end of the world was imminent. It was based on the incident of Herod's son going to Rome to obtain the formal title of "king" — a move which the local Jews opposed. In the story, a noble leaves his managers with some money. At his return for an accounting, those who increased the amount were rewarded. Those who had sat on the money were deprived of what they had. The point is that during this interim period of the Church, we are responsible to the Lord as to whether we preserve or expand our inheritance. We can apply both readings to ourselves and ask what our obligations to our parish might be. Do we see our church simply as a location for our own private religious experience or as a place where we are linked to a larger community of faith? This is the dynamic contained in today's parable: do we simply preserve our faith as a private possession or do we come to a community to enlarge and enrich our faith?

Point

Through our parish, we experience faith as more than doctrine and law. We experience it as fidelity to a concrete community of which we are a part.

THURSDAY — Thirty-Third Week of the Year
1 M 2:15-29   *Lk 19:41-44*

First Reading

In today's first reading, we have another response to this growing syncretism with Greek culture. We have seen the heroic responses of Eleazar and the mother of seven. Here,

Mattathias, an old priest, rises in fury and butchers the pagan priests thereby sparking a rebellion with his seven sons. It was a religious and political independence movement against oppression from without and disintegration from within. These rebels went to the desert and were joined by a group of holy men (hasidim) who would later separate from them. The political group went into guerilla warfare and won a few temporary victories. The religious group became the seed of the Essenes (a sort of isolated monastic community which had links with John the Baptist and provided a deep background for the Lord's early preaching). The political revolutionaries were successful for a time. The religious strand endured through the early Church and passed into Luke, John and Paul.

Gospel Reading

Jesus laments the coming destruction of Jerusalem. Jerusalem sought its ultimate salvation in political alliances alone. It would fall because it lacked internal strength. It was spiritually corrupt. It would endure in the Church only as a symbol. Political involvement as an instrument for the transformation of society is important but partial. It deals with external structures. The best of structures can be easily corrupted by the worst of people. A transformation within is also important. That is where Jerusalem failed. It is not only the external behaviors of our life that need renewal. We also need to be changed within. Our attitudes need rejuvenation. For that we require not behavior modification but the Holy Spirit of Christ.

Point

The impact of religion is more than political. Its effects are wider and deeper.

FRIDAY — Thirty-Third Week of the Year
1 M 4:36-37, 52-59   *Lk 19:45-48*

First Reading

In today's first reading, Mattathias' son, Judas Maccabeus, won the revolution. This is a time for the rededication of the Temple after the abomination (an altar to Zeus on which hogs had been sacrificed) had been removed. This ceremony is recalled today as Hanukkah, the feast of lights that is celebrated in home and synagogue. A menorah is lighted, one candle for each of eight days. Legend has it that the Maccabees ran out of oil for the Temple lights and discovered a single urn which lasted miraculously for eight days. It is a feast not only of the rededication of the Temple but also of Jews to Judaism.

Gospel Reading

The cleansing of the Temple is a gesture loaded with meaning. Jesus quotes Isaiah and Jeremiah. Isaiah (56) wrote: "I will bring foreigners to my holy mountain . . . for my house shall be called a house of prayer for all peoples." Jeremiah (7) wrote: "Here you are, putting trust in lies. Can you steal, murder, commit adultery and lie and then come into this house and say, 'We are safe. We can commit all these crimes again'? Has this temple become a hideout of thieves?"

The Lord condemns the exclusivity and the hypocrisy that had taken hold in the Temple. This forecasts what Jesus would become for all people. He would make His kingdom one for all people and nations, a place of justice where there would be no hypocrisy.

Point

We dedicate ourselves to the Lord. The greatest gift we have to set before Him is not a building but our lives.

SATURDAY — Thirty-Third Week of the Year
1 M 6:1-13   *Lk 20:27-40*

First Reading

The king Antiochus dies. It is a paradoxically just episode in the story of the Maccabees. A powerful and evil king is dead while the seemingly weak and holy tradition survives. In a broader sense, he represents a continuing threat to religion and faith in any age. Antiochus incarnates the tendency of political power to debase, use and blur the meaning of religious tradition. Antiochus sought to coopt the Jewish leaders. Only when that failed did he move to outright opposition. More dangerous than persecution, however, is the gradual blurring of the identity of a faith through a variety of financial, economic and political gratuities and incentives. Religions are seldom eliminated in a single stroke. Rather, they are eroded to death. It is very easy for a religious institution to win the whole world while losing its soul in the process. It is not only individuals but institutions that stand under the Lord's judgment.

Gospel Reading

To the Sadducees' disingenuous question about the wife of seven men and the status of her marriage in the next life, the Lord answers with a qualitatively different assertion. The next life is intrinsically different from the one we know here. He refers to the Book of Exodus and the experience of God which Moses had at the burning bush. This was the God of Abraham, Isaac and Jacob. In some way, these ancestors are alive in God's presence. Of course, they live through us in their effects, but Jesus speaks here of personal immortality. The same God who guaranteed the Exodus promises us eternal life as well. God's word is enough for our faith.

Point

Although we are promised eternal life, we can sell our souls here on earth and come to experience spiritual death before our time.

MONDAY — Thirty-Fourth Week of the Year
Dn 1:1-6, 8-20   *Lk 21:1-4*

First Reading

The Book of Daniel is an odd book of the Old Testament. It is a hybrid — half story and half prophecy. It concerns Daniel and the Babylonian court about 600 years before Christ. However, it was not written by Daniel but by someone living about a century and a half before Christ during the time of the Maccabees. That Maccabean crisis shaped the stories of Daniel to give encouragement to Jews who were being persecuted by Antiochus. Instead of pork, the heroes in today's reading eat vegetables and were protected. Fasting improved their appearance. The point of this story is to remain true to our traditions.

Gospel Reading

The widow in the little scene in today's Gospel reading is a symbol of the poor and dispossessed. The few pennies she contributed meant a great deal to her. It came from her heart and signified sincerity and authority. If the Book of Daniel reminds us that our traditions are important, that they are not passed on only by word of mouth but through ritual celebrations of every sort, then this reading reminds us that those traditions must be appropriated with sincerity and not simply by mechanical repetition. We are the ones who inherit traditions that we must bring to life in our own time. It is not a matter of repetition but of making ancient rituals instruments of our own personal communal experience.

Point

Traditions live through people and not through books.

TUESDAY — Thirty-Fourth Week of the Year
Dn 2:31-45   *Lk 21:5-11*

First Reading

This first reading from the Book of Daniel was written during the time of the Maccabees. Nebuchadnezzar has a dream which he wants his seers to interpret for him. Daniel alone is able to do so. This multipart statue, evidently designed by a committee, has decreasingly precious parts until its feet are composed of clay. Historically, the clay feet turn out to be none other than Antiochus. The point of the story is that power arrangements in the world are temporary. Antiochus also, therefore, is temporary while the kingdom of God endures. We can illustrate this from our own recollection of the world leaders who gathered for President Kennedy's funeral. The vast majority of them are gone from the world scene. The political problems that consumed us in those times seem to be light years away as new challenges confront us. Yet, the root problems that face God's kingdom — sin and evil — continue to conflict with grace and holiness and remain the motor forces that push history forward.

Gospel Reading

Jesus makes an identical point in today's Gospel reading. The disciples had been admiring the engineering marvel that the Temple was. The Lord warns them not to put their trust in the stones. These particular buildings will disappear. It is the kingdom of God that endures. The rule of Christ continues. We can see this again from our own experience if we consider the changes that have occurred in Church leadership since the time of President Kennedy's funeral. Many things in the Church have changed and will continue to change. This is not a new phenomenon. Shifts occurred in the Church during the twenties, thirties, forties, fifties and so on. It is important that we not turn Church or State into a God. They are instruments of God's design. The power arrangements and cultural patterns will change but embedded beneath all this is the enduring kingdom of God.

Point

We should recall that in all the chaos that runs through our life, we all have one foot in the enduring kingdom of God.

WEDNESDAY — Thirty-Fourth Week of the Year
Dn 5:1-6, 13-14, 16-17, 23-28   *Lk 21:12-19*

First Reading

King Belshazzar gave a feast that has forever become synonymous with excess and profanation. During the celebration in which he uses vessels plundered from the Jerusalem Temple, handwriting appears on the wall. Daniel interprets the words for him, the gist of which was: "This party is over!" The Persians were about to take over the Babylonian kingdom. Thus the fate of Belshazzar was sealed. There are several messages in this story. First, God is in control of history: not simply ecclesiastical history but secular and economic history as well. God's judgment is present in oil prices, interest rates,

rates of exchange, the strength of the dollar, Third World debt, power politics, the arms race and the shifting economic alliances of nations. Secondly, there is retribution in some form for the profanation of God's people, Temple and rituals. An attack on the people of God is a sacrilege which the Lord will not allow to go unpunished. Thirdly, the judgment may come slowly through deterioration or quickly through collapse. God's judgment exists in individual lives as well as in the broad contours of history.

Gospel Reading

Jesus speaks about persecution that will befall not only the early Church but Christians in every age. We are all very familiar with the opposition that staggered the first Christians. Perhaps we are not as familiar with the persecutions that beset the Church today on many continents. In Africa, Europe and South America the roll of martyrs continues to grow. In our own country, the persecution is more subtle. We are subject to a barrage of stereotyping through the media, attacks upon the institution of the Church and its bishops, and career and professional discrimination against Catholics. The age of persecution is by no means over. The Colosseum is now worldwide: boardrooms, television studios, classrooms, government offices and legislatures.

Point

Both the presence of God and the persecution of the Church can take many subtle and unanticipated forms.

THURSDAY — Thirty-Fourth Week of the Year
Dn 6:12-28   *Lk 21:20-28*

First Reading

King Belshazzar is gone from the scene. We now have

King Darius, a Persian. Daniel is still an exile. The king decreed that no foreign gods are to be served. Daniel remains true to his traditions and is therefore thrown into the lions' den. When the king sees that Daniel is unharmed because of the power of his God, he orders him to be released and his place to be taken by his opponents. All of this presages the edict of his successor allowing the Jews to return to Jerusalem after the exile. The message of this story is again directed to Jews at the time of King Antiochus urging them to remain true to their traditions. Their God will protect them.

Gospel Reading

Jesus speaks about the coming destruction of Jerusalem and the end of the world. The terrible signs are apocalyptic indicators of the new direction which creation is about to take. It is critical to remember that the purpose of judgment in the Bible is not only reprisal. The coming destruction is to be a re-creation. Whatever is sinful will be eliminated as the reign of God's will descends. Utter destruction is not the purpose or end of the story. The Son of Man will come with deliverance for His people. This is the note with which Jesus concludes these dire warnings. When these things begin to occur, we can be sure that deliverance and liberation are near. How one looks at the last things is in direct proportion to the conduct of one's life. If our life has been in accord with the Lord's will, His second coming in history or at death will be a welcoming. If our life has been in opposition to the Lord, His coming in history or at the end of our life will be a rejection.

Point

God will deliver His own people.

FRIDAY — Thirty-Fourth Week of the Year
Dn 7:2-14   *Lk 21:29-33*

First Reading

The Book of Daniel's prophetic passages have provided a great deal of material for fiery evangelical preachers and for people with fertile imaginations who manage to read every sort of contemporary event and modern trend into them. We must recall as we interpret these sections that the Book of Daniel was written for people at the time of King Antiochus. It has, of course, a universal message but we must remain, first of all, true to its original intent as best we can discern it. The four beasts represent the four kingdoms that overtook Judah: Babylonians, Medes, Persians and Greeks. The ten horns on the Greek beast signified the Greek rulers with the little horn standing for none other than Antiochus. After the emergence of this final beast, the court of God's judgment is convened and the beasts are destroyed. The Christian tradition has seen in the "son of man" a prophecy of the Lord Jesus to whom is given universal control.

Gospel Reading

Jesus also speaks in apocalyptic terms. He emphasizes the signs that the kingdom is near. His words are true and worthy of trust. The Lord's reference to the present generation indicates that the kingdom is transtemporal. It is available to every person on the spiritual and sacramental level. There will come a time at the end of history when that kingdom will be made obvious and will be acknowledged by all. For now, we live in a time of liturgy. Nevertheless, the reign and power of God is not something that is merely symbolic. It is a real power that is accessible to us now.

Point

The kingdom of Christ is stronger than any temporal kingdom.

SATURDAY — Thirty-Fourth Week of the Year
Dn 7:15-27   *Lk 21:34-36*

First Reading

The vision of Daniel is explained. It is important to remember that the Book of Daniel was written for Jews sorely tested by King Antiochus. These visions reminded them that his reign would be temporary. History was not absurd; everything was known to God. Not only would final victory be given to God's holy ones but evil would at some point be finally eliminated. This was the significance of the Book of Daniel to Jews about a century and a half before Christ. It has a message for every age. We cannot provide exact equivalences for every item of his visions in our own time. It is sufficient to recall that the meaning of the beasts — opposition to the reign of God — is that tension will beset the Church's life until the very end. We must not think that the fact of persecution, in whatever form, means that somehow we have fallen from God's grace. That antithesis between Church and world is systemic and will not disappear until the Lord comes in His glory to bring human efforts at last to a final, peaceful and successful end.

Gospel Reading

Jesus warns His disciples not to become bloated with contentment as though the political compromises we can arrange to secure the Church can provide safety from covert forms of persecution. Persecution, attack and resentment are the lot of disciples as it was of the Lord. The fact that we are opposed does not preclude our seeking avenues of contact and unity with others. We must constantly be aware, however, that we have a clear, vivid identity, mission and message that is uniquely ours. It was not evolved but entrusted to us. It cannot be compromised or sold away. That mission and identity with its glory and its pain is forever ours. It is the mission and message begun by Christ.

Point

Persecution, in any form, reminds us that we are to live as a Church in the shadow of the Cross. It is our built-in reminder as well of the glory and grace of the Resurrection.